The Momentum Mindset

Dr. J

The Momentum Mindset

Published by Dr. J

Table of Contents

Introduction

The book which you now hold in your hands, *The Momentum Mindset*, can change your life if you'll allow it. For more than twenty-five years as a spiritual teacher and leading manifestation coach, I have witnessed firsthand how lives are transformed through the shift toward more dynamic mindsets. Everything begins within the mind. It's time for you to unleash the Divine Mind within you and achieve the life of your dreams.

Everything begins within the mind, a vast and intricate landscape where thoughts take root, ideas sprout, and dreams are born. It is within this enigmatic realm that the seeds of creativity are sown, and the tapestry of reality is woven.

The mind is a boundless canvas, where the brushstrokes of imagination paint the picture of our lives. It is the epicenter of our perceptions, where we interpret the world around us, shaping our beliefs and shaping our understanding of the universe. From the smallest of actions to the grandest of achievements, everything we do, every choice we make, originates from the depths of our consciousness.

The power of the mind is unparalleled, for it is the source of our motivations and aspirations. It is here that we forge our desires and set our goals, driving us forward on our individual journeys. It is also within the mind that fears and doubts can take root, hindering our progress and limiting our potential. The mind is both a battleground and a sanctuary, where we grapple with our inner demons and seek solace in moments of introspection.

In the realm of science and innovation, the mind is the crucible of discovery. It is where scientists conceive groundbreaking theories, inventors envision revolutionary technologies, and artists create masterpieces that transcend time. The mind's capacity to imagine the unimaginable has led humanity to explore the depths of the oceans, the vastness of space, and the intricacies of the subatomic world. It is the birthplace of revolutions, both intellectual and societal, shaping the course of history.

But the mind is not just a wellspring of intellectual prowess; it is also the crucible of empathy and compassion. It is here that we cultivate our capacity to understand the feelings and perspectives of others, fostering connections and building bridges between diverse cultures and communities. It is within the mind that we forge bonds of love, friendship, and solidarity, extending our reach beyond the confines of our physical existence.

In the pursuit of self-improvement, the mind is our greatest ally and our fiercest adversary. It is through mindfulness and self-reflection that we strive to overcome our limitations and evolve as individuals. Yet, it is also within the mind that we grapple with self-doubt, insecurity, and the endless quest for self-acceptance.

So everything truly begins within the mind. It is the fertile soil from which the seeds of human experience take root and grow. Our thoughts, emotions, and aspirations are the fruits of this remarkable landscape, and it is through the exploration and nurturing of our inner world that we embark on the profound journey of self-discovery and transformation. The mind is the genesis of our reality, the epicenter of our consciousness, and the wellspring of our existence.

Within the confines of our minds, there exists a dynamic interplay between the conscious and the subconscious, a complex dance of thoughts and emotions that shape our perception of the world. It is in this intricate choreography that the seeds of innovation are planted and where the roots of tradition find sustenance. Our thoughts are like seeds scattered upon the fertile soil of our consciousness, and our actions are the harvest they yield.

The mind is a treasure trove of memories, a vast library where every experience, every emotion, every sensation is cataloged and stored. It is within this repository that we revisit moments of joy and nostalgia, draw lessons from past mistakes, and forge a sense of identity. Our memories are the threads that weave the tapestry of our personal history, binding us to our past and shaping our future.

The power of visualization, a gift of the mind, cannot be underestimated. Through the mind's eye, we can imagine a better world, envision our goals, and chart a course toward them. It is through this mental rehearsal that athletes prepare for their competitions, artists create their masterpieces, and individuals strive to manifest their dreams into reality. The mind is the canvas upon which we paint the portrait of our desires, and with each stroke of imagination, we inch closer to our aspirations.

Emotions, too, are a product of the mind's alchemy. Love, joy, sorrow, anger—all find their origin within our thoughts and perceptions. The mind's ability to conjure a spectrum of emotions is a testament to its complexity and influence over our lives. It is through understanding and managing our emotions that we navigate the intricate web of human relationships, forging connections and finding meaning in our interactions with others.

The mind is a crucible of learning, where curiosity fuels the fire of knowledge. It is through inquiry and exploration that we expand the boundaries of our understanding, pushing the frontiers of science and philosophy. The insatiable hunger for knowledge that resides within the mind has propelled humanity forward, fostering innovation and progress.

However, the mind is not without its shadows. It can be a realm of doubt and self-criticism, where inner demons lurk, ready to sabotage our confidence and potential. Yet, it is also within the mind that we find the resilience to confront these shadows, to conquer our fears, and to emerge stronger and wiser.

In essence, everything we experience, create, and aspire to begins within the mind. It is the crucible of human existence, the forge of creativity, and the repository of our hopes and fears. Our thoughts, emotions, and memories are the building blocks of our lives, and it is through the constant exploration and nurturing of our inner world that we find meaning, purpose, and the endless possibilities of the human spirit. The mind is both the origin and the compass of our journey through the labyrinth of existence, guiding us as we navigate the complex terrain of life.

The mind's influence extends far beyond the boundaries of our individual lives; it shapes the collective consciousness of societies and civilizations. It is through the collective minds of people that cultures are formed, traditions are upheld, and social norms are established. The shared thoughts, beliefs, and values of a community emerge from the amalgamation of individual minds, creating a tapestry of shared identity and purpose.

Philosophers and thinkers throughout history have pondered the nature of reality and the mind's role in shaping it. From Plato's allegory of the cave to Descartes' famous declaration, "I think, therefore I am," the philosophical exploration of the mind's power has been a central theme in human thought. These inquiries have not only deepened our understanding of the mind but have also paved the way for scientific and technological advancements.

The mind's creative potential has given rise to art, literature, music, and countless forms of expression. Artists channel their innermost thoughts and emotions into their work, offering glimpses into the human experience that resonate across time and culture. Writers craft intricate narratives that transport readers to far-off worlds or evoke deep introspection. Musicians compose symphonies that stir the soul, transcending language and speaking directly to the heart.

The mind's role in decision-making is paramount. Every choice we make, whether significant or trivial, is a product of our cognitive processes. It is through reasoning, weighing pros and cons, and considering the consequences that we arrive at decisions that shape our lives. The mind's capacity for rational thought is what enables us to plan for the future, set goals, and work toward achieving them.

Moreover, the mind is the crucible of empathy and compassion, the foundation of our capacity to connect with others on a profound level. It is through our ability to understand and relate to the thoughts and emotions of others that we build bonds of empathy and forge deep, meaningful relationships. This interconnectedness is what makes society function harmoniously, fostering cooperation and mutual support.

In the realm of science and innovation, the mind's insatiable curiosity and thirst for knowledge drive us to explore the mysteries of the universe. Scientific breakthroughs, technological advancements, and medical discoveries all begin as questions in the minds of scientists and researchers. The mind's capacity to question, experiment, and analyze is what propels us forward, solving complex problems and improving the human condition.

In the grand tapestry of existence, the mind is the weaver, the artist, and the philosopher. It is the force that propels us forward, the compass that guides us through the labyrinth of life, and the repository of our past, present, and future. Everything we perceive, create, and aspire to starts within the mind—a boundless, ever-evolving landscape where the human spirit explores the depths of consciousness and finds the limitless potential within itself. It is through the ceaseless exploration and nurturing of this inner world that we, as individuals and as a collective, continue to evolve, innovate, and chart the course of our shared destiny.

The mind's influence extends even further, penetrating the very fabric of human society and shaping the course of history. It is within the collective minds of communities and nations that ideologies are forged, political movements are born, and revolutions are ignited. Ideas have the power to spark social change, and it is the collective mind that propels societies toward progress or stagnation.

Throughout history, visionaries and leaders have harnessed the power of the mind to inspire change on a grand scale. Thinkers like Mahatma Gandhi, Martin Luther King Jr., and Nelson Mandela used their intellect and moral convictions to challenge oppressive systems and advocate for justice and equality. Their words and actions, rooted in the power of the mind, led to transformative social and political movements that reshaped the world.

The mind is also the wellspring of innovation in business and technology. Entrepreneurs and inventors conceive groundbreaking ideas within the recesses of their thoughts. These ideas are nurtured, refined, and brought to fruition through the application of knowledge, dedication, and hard work. From the invention of the light bulb to the creation of the internet, the mind's capacity for innovation has revolutionized industries and changed the way we live.

The mind's ability to adapt and learn is a fundamental aspect of human nature. It is through education and the transmission of knowledge from one generation to the next that civilizations progress. The mind is both the student and the teacher, absorbing the wisdom of the past and passing on accumulated knowledge to future generations. This continuous exchange of ideas and insights fuels the advancement of human culture and science.

Furthermore, the mind's connection to health and well-being is undeniable. The field of psychology explores the intricate workings of the mind and its impact on mental and emotional health. Through therapy, counseling, and mindfulness practices, individuals learn to navigate the complexities of their own minds, overcoming challenges and achieving a sense of balance and fulfillment.

In the realm of spirituality and philosophy, the mind is a central focus. It is through contemplation, meditation, and self-reflection that individuals seek deeper understanding and connection with the spiritual dimensions of existence. The mind becomes a tool for exploring the mysteries of consciousness, the nature of existence, and the meaning of life itself.

The mind is the epicenter of human experience, the origin of creativity, the catalyst for change, and the guardian of knowledge. It is the source of our thoughts, emotions, and aspirations, and it shapes the world both individually and collectively. From the most profound philosophical ponderings to the most practical innovations, everything that defines human existence begins within the mind. It is a boundless frontier of potential, an ever-evolving landscape of consciousness, and a testament to the incredible capabilities of the human spirit. The mind is not only where everything begins, but it is also where the possibilities for the future are limitless, awaiting exploration and realization.

As we delve deeper into the profound influence of the mind, it becomes evident that each of us possesses the key to unlock our full potential. The power to shift our mindset from passive to dynamic lies within our grasp. The mind is not a static entity; it is malleable, adaptable, and responsive to our intentions. By harnessing this incredible capacity for change, we can propel ourselves toward the realization of our goals and aspirations.

The first step in this transformative journey is self-awareness. We must become intimately acquainted with the workings of our own minds. By observing our thoughts, recognizing our patterns of thinking, and acknowledging our beliefs and limitations, we gain insight into the landscape of our consciousness. This awareness serves as the foundation upon which we can build a more dynamic mindset.

With self-awareness as our compass, we can begin to challenge and reshape our thought patterns. Often, we find ourselves trapped in self-limiting beliefs, doubting our abilities, or succumbing to negative thinking. However, the mind is not beholden to these limitations. We have the power to question and replace unproductive thoughts with empowering ones. Instead of dwelling on obstacles, we can focus on opportunities. Rather than fixating on failure, we can embrace the lessons it offers. By consciously choosing our thoughts and reframing our perspective, we shift from a static mindset to a dynamic one.

A dynamic mindset is characterized by resilience and adaptability. It thrives on challenges and views setbacks as stepping stones to growth. This mindset understands that failure is not a destination but a detour on the path to success. It is unafraid of change and embraces it as an opportunity for learning and innovation.

Moreover, a dynamic mindset is goal-oriented. It sets clear objectives and formulates plans to achieve them. It understands that dreams and aspirations become attainable when we break them down into actionable steps. It is fueled by determination and persistence, for it knows that the road to success is often paved with hard work and dedication.

As we cultivate a dynamic mindset, we tap into the vast reserves of creativity and innovation within us. The mind, when freed from the constraints of self-doubt and complacency, becomes a wellspring of ideas and solutions. It encourages us to explore new possibilities, take calculated risks, and push the boundaries of what we thought was achievable.

In this dynamic state of mind, we discover the power to turn obstacles into opportunities, setbacks into comebacks, and dreams into reality. It is a mindset that propels us forward, enabling us to face life's challenges with confidence and grace. It is the key to unlocking our untapped potential and harnessing the boundless energy of the mind to achieve our goals.

The mind is a powerful force that can be harnessed and directed toward the realization of our deepest desires. By shifting our mindset from passive to dynamic, we open the doors to a world of possibilities. It is within our reach to transform our thoughts, overcome limitations, and chart a course toward success. As you read these words, remember that the mind is your greatest ally, and with determination, self-awareness, and a dynamic mindset, you hold the power to shape your destiny and accomplish extraordinary feats. Embrace the dynamic potential within you and set forth on a journey of self-discovery and achievement, for the mind is the canvas upon which your dreams can become a vibrant reality.

To fully embrace and actualize the potential of a dynamic mindset, we must also recognize the importance of resilience in the face of adversity. Life is replete with challenges, setbacks, and moments of uncertainty. However, it is the dynamic mindset that equips us with the mental fortitude to weather these storms and emerge stronger on the other side.

Resilience, within the context of a dynamic mindset, means not only bouncing back from setbacks but also using adversity as a catalyst for growth. It acknowledges that failures and obstacles are not signs of inadequacy but opportunities for improvement. When we encounter challenges, a dynamic mindset encourages us to view them as tests of our resolve and as chances to refine our strategies.

Moreover, a dynamic mindset thrives on adaptability. It understands that the world is in constant flux, and those who can adapt to change are the ones who succeed. In an ever-evolving landscape, a rigid and inflexible mindset can become a barrier to progress. However, by embracing change as a natural part of life, we open ourselves up to new possibilities and innovations.

Another crucial aspect of a dynamic mindset is the ability to set and pursue goals with unwavering determination. Goals serve as beacons of purpose, guiding our actions and decisions. A dynamic mindset is goal-driven, breaking down aspirations into manageable steps and celebrating small victories along the way. It recognizes that the path to success may be long and challenging, but the journey is as important as the destination.

Furthermore, a dynamic mindset is characterized by a growth-oriented perspective. It understands that intelligence, talents, and abilities can be developed over time through effort and learning. This belief in the potential for growth fosters a hunger for knowledge and an eagerness to embrace new skills and experiences. It is a mindset that thrives on continuous self-improvement.

In cultivating a dynamic mindset, it is essential to surround oneself with positivity and support. Environments and relationships that nurture optimism, encouragement, and constructive feedback are instrumental in maintaining a resilient and growth-focused mindset. Connecting with mentors, peers, and communities that share similar goals and values can provide invaluable support on the journey toward success.

Ultimately, a dynamic mindset is not a static destination but a continuous process of self-discovery and growth. It is a lifelong commitment to harnessing the incredible potential within the mind and channeling it toward achieving dreams and aspirations. It is a reminder that the power to shape our destiny, overcome challenges, and accomplish extraordinary feats resides within each of us.

The dynamic mindset is not a mere concept but a practical approach to life. It is the realization that we have the capacity to shift our thoughts, behaviors, and perspectives to navigate the complexities of existence effectively. With self-awareness, resilience, adaptability, goal-setting, and a growth-oriented perspective, we can unleash the full potential of our minds. Embrace the dynamic mindset as a powerful tool to propel yourself toward success, fulfillment, and a life filled with limitless possibilities.

Remember that within the boundless landscape of your mind lies the key to shaping your destiny and achieving the extraordinary.

Allow me to introduce you to John, a man whose life underwent a profound transformation through a dynamic shift in his mindset. John's story serves as an inspiring testament to the incredible power of the human mind.

John had spent most of his life in a state of complacency, working a monotonous job that provided stability but left him unfulfilled. He had dreams of pursuing a career in music, but self-doubt and the fear of failure had kept those aspirations locked away in the recesses of his mind. He had resigned himself to a life of routine, convinced that his dreams were beyond reach.

However, a pivotal moment in John's life ignited a spark within him. He attended a motivational seminar where he heard speakers share their own stories of transformation and success achieved through a dynamic mindset. It was as if a switch had been flipped in his consciousness. He realized that the only thing holding him back was his own limiting beliefs and fear of failure.

With newfound determination, John embarked on a journey of self-discovery. He began by challenging his negative thought patterns and replacing them with positive affirmations. He reminded himself daily that he had the potential to achieve his dreams and that setbacks were merely opportunities for growth.

One of the most significant shifts in John's mindset was his attitude towards failure. Instead of viewing failures as insurmountable obstacles, he started seeing them as stepping stones to success. He understood that each setback provided valuable lessons and that resilience and perseverance were the keys to progress.

John also set clear, achievable goals for himself in the field of music. He started practicing diligently, honing his skills, and seeking opportunities to perform. He joined a local band, collaborated with other musicians, and began to build a network within the music industry. He understood that his dreams required both dedication and action.

As John continued on his journey, he encountered challenges and setbacks, just as he had anticipated. But he faced them head-on with unwavering determination and resilience. Instead of giving in to self-doubt, he used these moments as opportunities for self-improvement. His dynamic mindset allowed him to adapt to changing circumstances, learn from his experiences, and keep moving forward.

Over time, John's efforts began to bear fruit. He started receiving recognition for his musical talent, performing at local venues, and even recording his own songs. His music touched the hearts of others and inspired them to pursue their own dreams. John had not only transformed his own life but had become a source of inspiration for those around him.

John's story is a powerful reminder that a dynamic mindset has the potential to reshape our lives in extraordinary ways. Through self-awareness, resilience, adaptability, and goal-setting, he shifted from a life of complacency to one of purpose and fulfillment. His journey illustrates that it is never too late to pursue our passions, and the only limits that truly exist are the ones we place on ourselves.

As you reflect on John's story, remember that the power to change your life through a mindshift lies within your own mind. Embrace the potential for growth, challenge self-limiting beliefs, and take actionable steps toward your dreams. Like John, you have the capacity to transform your life and become a source of inspiration for others on their own journeys of self-discovery and achievement.

John's story continued to evolve as he continued his journey of self-discovery and personal growth. His dynamic mindset had not only propelled him toward a successful music career but had also influenced various aspects of his life.

One of the most remarkable changes in John was his newfound sense of self-confidence. The realization that he could overcome challenges and setbacks had bolstered his self-esteem. He carried himself with assurance, which not only impacted his professional life but also improved his personal relationships. John's friends and family noticed the transformation in him, admiring his resilience and determination.

As John's music career gained momentum, he decided to give back to the community that had supported him on his journey. He started volunteering his time and talent to mentor aspiring musicians, especially those who lacked the resources and opportunities he once did. John believed that everyone had the potential to achieve their dreams if they embraced a dynamic mindset.

His mentoring efforts soon evolved into workshops and seminars where he shared his own story of transformation and the principles of a dynamic mindset. His words resonated with many, inspiring them to break free from their self-imposed limitations and pursue their passions with vigor. John's impact reached far beyond his music, as he became a motivational speaker and advocate for personal growth and empowerment.

In his personal life, John also experienced positive changes. His relationships with family and friends deepened as he became more open and authentic. He understood the importance of surrounding himself with a supportive network, and he encouraged those around him to pursue their own dreams. John's dynamic mindset had not only transformed his life but had become a source of inspiration and motivation for others.

As the years passed, John's music career continued to thrive. He released albums, performed on national stages, and achieved recognition as a respected artist. Yet, he remained grounded and humble, never forgetting the journey that had brought him to where he was.

John's story serves as a powerful reminder that a dynamic mindset can lead to not only personal success but also a profound impact on others and the community. His transformation from a life of complacency to one of purpose and contribution illustrates the ripple effect that occurs when one person embraces the power of their own mind.

John's story encourages us to reflect on our own lives and consider the incredible potential for growth that resides within each of us. Through self-awareness, resilience, adaptability, and goal-setting, we have the ability to shift our mindset and create positive changes that extend beyond ourselves. Whether it's in pursuing a passion, helping others, or achieving personal goals, we can draw inspiration from John's journey and embark on our own transformative path. As you continue your own life's journey, remember that a dynamic mindset has the power to shape not only your destiny but also the world around you.

John's story is a vivid illustration of how the Law of Attraction played a significant role in his transformation. The Law of Attraction posits that like attracts like, suggesting that our thoughts and beliefs have a direct influence on the events and circumstances that manifest in our lives. John's dynamic mindset was, in essence, a powerful application of the Law of Attraction.

When John shifted his mindset from doubt and complacency to one of self-belief and determination, he inadvertently activated the Law of Attraction in his favor. By consistently focusing on his dream of a successful music career, he was sending out positive vibrations into the universe. This shift in his mental landscape not only altered his internal dialogue but also began to draw into his life the people, opportunities, and resources that aligned with his aspirations.

As John started believing in his dreams and goals, his confidence radiated from him. He attracted like-minded individuals who shared his passion for music and self-improvement.

Collaborations and opportunities began to present themselves as he networked and connected with those who believed in his vision. It was as if the universe conspired to support his journey because his thoughts and intentions were in harmony with his desires.

Moreover, the Law of Attraction also influenced John's decision-making and actions. He became more attuned to opportunities that aligned with his goals, and he seized them with enthusiasm and purpose. This proactive approach further solidified his belief that his dreams were achievable and within reach.

John's story is a testament to the idea that our beliefs and thoughts can shape our reality. When we genuinely believe in our dreams and visualize our success, we not only alter our mindset but also set into motion a chain of events that brings us closer to our aspirations. It is as if the universe responds to our intentions and aligns circumstances in our favor.

In the context of the Law of Attraction, John's dynamic mindset was a catalyst for his success. It was the unwavering belief in his abilities and dreams that attracted the right people, opportunities, and experiences into his life. As he continued to visualize his goals and take inspired action, he witnessed his dreams manifest into reality.

John's story serves as a compelling example of how the Law of Attraction can be harnessed to achieve one's goals and aspirations. It underscores the importance of not only shifting one's mindset but also embracing the power of positive thinking and belief. As you reflect on John's journey, remember that your thoughts and beliefs have the potential to shape your reality. By aligning your mindset with your desires and taking inspired action, you can unlock the transformative power of the Law of Attraction in your own life, just as John did in his pursuit of a fulfilling music career and a life of purpose.

In the journey of life, there is a force more potent than any external circumstance, more influential than luck or fate – it's the unwavering belief in our own abilities. Belief, in its purest form, is the catalyst that can propel us to achieve the extraordinary, overcome seemingly insurmountable obstacles, and carve a path toward success and fulfillment. It is the cornerstone of personal development and the driving force behind transformative change.

Belief in our abilities lays the foundation for achievement. It serves as the bedrock upon which we construct our goals, dreams, and aspirations. When we believe in ourselves, we set the stage for success because we have faith that our efforts will yield positive results. This self-assuredness allows us to venture into uncharted territory, take calculated risks, and pursue opportunities with confidence.

Consider the stories of accomplished individuals throughout history. From inventors like Thomas Edison to visionary leaders like Nelson Mandela, their unwavering belief in their abilities propelled them to achieve remarkable feats. Edison once famously said, "I have not failed. I've just found 10,000 ways that won't work." His belief in his ability to innovate and solve problems led to groundbreaking inventions that changed the world.

Belief is the antidote to self-doubt, that insidious voice within us that whispers tales of inadequacy and fear. When we believe in our abilities, we silence the doubting voices and replace them with a chorus of self-assurance. This shift in perspective allows us to confront challenges with resilience and unwavering determination.

It's important to acknowledge that self-doubt is a natural part of the human experience. We all face moments of uncertainty and insecurity. However, it is our belief in our abilities that enables us to transcend these moments and press forward. The realization that we have the power to overcome self-doubt and grow from it is a profound testament to the strength of belief.

Belief in our abilities is the engine of progress. It fuels our ambitions and propels us toward continuous improvement. When we believe in our capacity to learn, adapt, and evolve, we embrace challenges as opportunities for growth rather than as roadblocks. This growth mindset, as coined by psychologist Carol Dweck, is a powerful perspective that encourages us to view setbacks as stepping stones to success.

In the world of entrepreneurship, for example, belief in one's abilities is often the driving force behind innovation and risk-taking.

Entrepreneurs like Steve Jobs and Elon Musk believed in their visions for groundbreaking products and technologies, even when faced with skepticism and adversity. Their unwavering belief not only led to the creation of iconic companies like Apple and SpaceX but also transformed entire industries.

Belief in our abilities is the driving force behind personal growth, achievement, and resilience. It empowers us to set ambitious goals, conquer self-doubt, and overcome obstacles. As we cultivate and nurture this belief, we unlock the potential for transformative change in our lives. Remember, your abilities are not limited by external circumstances or the opinions of others. The most powerful belief you can hold is the one in yourself. Embrace it, nurture it, and watch as it propels you toward a future of limitless possibilities.

Belief in our abilities not only impacts our own lives but also has a ripple effect on those around us. When we believe in ourselves, we inspire others to do the same. Our confidence becomes infectious, encouraging our friends, family, and colleagues to pursue their own dreams and goals.

Imagine a workplace where individuals believe in their abilities and collaborate with unwavering determination. The result is a culture of innovation, where teams tackle challenges with confidence and creativity. Belief in abilities can foster a positive work environment that thrives on growth and achievement.

In our personal lives, our belief in our abilities can be a source of motivation and inspiration for our loved ones. When we model self-belief, we teach those around us the power of resilience, determination, and the pursuit of their own dreams.

In the grand tapestry of human potential, belief in our abilities is the thread that weaves our dreams into reality. It is the driving force that propels us to set ambitious goals, overcome self-doubt, and embrace challenges with resilience. As we cultivate and nurture this belief, we not only transform our own lives but also inspire those around us.

The journey of self-belief is not a solitary one; it is a collective endeavor that ripples through our communities and society at large. By embracing the power of belief in our abilities, we unlock the doors to personal growth, achievement, and a future filled with limitless possibilities.

So, let us embark on this transformative journey with unwavering self-assurance, for our belief in our abilities is the key to unlocking our full potential and creating a brighter, more empowered future for ourselves and for those we touch along the way. Embrace your abilities, believe in them, and let them lead you to the extraordinary.

In the grand tapestry of human potential, belief in our abilities is the thread that weaves our dreams into reality. It is the driving force that propels us to set ambitious goals, overcome self-doubt, and embrace challenges with resilience. As we cultivate and nurture this belief, we not only transform our own lives but also inspire those around us.

The journey of self-belief is not a solitary one; it is a collective endeavor that ripples through our communities and society at large. By embracing the power of belief in our abilities, we unlock the doors to personal growth, achievement, and a future filled with limitless possibilities.

So, let us embark on this transformative journey with unwavering self-assurance, for our belief in our abilities is the key to unlocking our full potential and creating a brighter, more empowered future for ourselves and for those we touch along the way. Embrace your abilities, believe in them, and let them lead you to the extraordinary.

When we believe in our abilities, we embrace a mindset of possibility rather than limitation. We recognize that our potential is not bound by circumstances or external factors. Instead, it is a force that resides within us, waiting to be harnessed and directed toward our goals and aspirations.

Consider the journey of individuals who have made significant contributions to various fields. Scientists who believed in their ability to solve complex problems and unlock the mysteries of the universe, artists who believed in their creative vision and pushed the boundaries of their craft, and entrepreneurs who believed in their innovative ideas and reshaped industries – they all shared a common thread of unwavering self-belief.

Self-belief not only influences our mindset but also shapes our behaviors and actions. When we believe in our abilities, we are more likely to take initiative, set ambitious goals, and persist in the face of challenges. This proactive approach to life leads to personal growth and accomplishment.

Furthermore, belief in our abilities enhances our resilience. It provides us with the mental fortitude to bounce back from setbacks and failures. Instead of seeing obstacles as insurmountable, we view them as opportunities for learning and growth. This resilience allows us to adapt to changing circumstances and continue pursuing our goals with unwavering determination.

Belief in our abilities is a transformative force that shapes our mindset, behaviors, and actions. It is the cornerstone of personal growth and achievement, enabling us to pursue our dreams with unwavering determination and resilience. As you continue on your journey of self-discovery and self-belief, remember that your potential knows no bounds. Embrace your abilities, believe in them, and let them guide you toward a future filled with limitless possibilities.

In the grand tapestry of human potential, belief in our abilities is the thread that weaves our dreams into reality. It is the driving force that propels us to set ambitious goals, overcome self-doubt, and embrace challenges with resilience. As we cultivate and nurture this belief, we not only transform our own lives but also inspire those around us.

The journey of self-belief is not a solitary one; it is a collective endeavor that ripples through our communities and society at large. By embracing the power of belief in our abilities, we unlock the doors to personal growth, achievement, and a future filled with limitless possibilities.

So, let us embark on this transformative journey with unwavering self-assurance, for our belief in our abilities is the key to unlocking our full potential and creating a brighter, more empowered future for ourselves and for those we touch along the way. Embrace your abilities, believe in them, and let them lead you to the extraordinary.

When we believe in our abilities, we embrace a mindset of possibility rather than limitation. We recognize that our potential is not bound by circumstances or external factors. Instead, it is a force that resides within us, waiting to be harnessed and directed toward our goals and aspirations.

Consider the journey of individuals who have made significant contributions to various fields. Scientists who believed in their ability to solve complex problems and unlock the mysteries of the universe, artists who believed in their creative vision and pushed the boundaries of their craft, and entrepreneurs who believed in their innovative ideas and reshaped industries – they all shared a common thread of unwavering self-belief.

Self-belief not only influences our mindset but also shapes our behaviors and actions. When we believe in our abilities, we are more likely to take initiative, set ambitious goals, and persist in the face of challenges. This proactive approach to life leads to personal growth and accomplishment.

Furthermore, belief in our abilities enhances our resilience. It provides us with the mental fortitude to bounce back from setbacks and failures. Instead of seeing obstacles as insurmountable, we view them as opportunities for learning and growth. This resilience allows us to adapt to changing circumstances and continue pursuing our goals with unwavering determination.

In conclusion, belief in our abilities is a transformative force that shapes our mindset, behaviors, and actions. It is the cornerstone of personal growth and achievement, enabling us to pursue our dreams with unwavering determination and resilience. As you continue on your journey of self-discovery and self-belief, remember that your potential knows no bounds. Embrace your abilities, believe in them, and let them guide you toward a future filled with limitless possibilities.

Belief in our abilities is not just a solitary endeavor; it has a profound impact on the world around us. When we embrace our own potential and believe in our capabilities, we become beacons of inspiration for others. Our confidence becomes infectious, encouraging those in our circle to reach for their own dreams and to believe in themselves.

Think about the ripple effect of belief in our abilities within families. Parents who believe in their children's potential and encourage them to pursue their passions instill a sense of self-belief that can last a lifetime. These children, in turn, grow up with the confidence to tackle challenges, set ambitious goals, and make a positive impact on the world.

In educational settings, teachers who believe in their students' abilities can ignite a spark of self-confidence that transcends the classroom. Students who feel supported and encouraged to believe in themselves often excel academically and go on to achieve remarkable feats in their chosen fields.

Belief in our abilities is also a powerful driver of innovation and progress. Entrepreneurs and inventors who have unwavering faith in their ideas push the boundaries of what is possible. They create groundbreaking technologies, services, and solutions that transform industries and improve the lives of countless people.

Consider the story of Elon Musk, a visionary entrepreneur known for his belief in the potential of sustainable energy and space exploration. Musk's steadfast self-belief has driven the creation of companies like SpaceX and Tesla, which have revolutionized the aerospace and automotive industries. His innovations inspire not only those in his companies but also countless individuals worldwide who now see the possibilities of a sustainable future and space exploration.

In leadership roles, belief in one's abilities can have a cascading effect on teams and organizations. Leaders who lead with confidence and believe in their abilities inspire their teams to achieve exceptional results. They create an environment where employees feel valued and motivated to contribute their best.

The belief in our abilities can also foster a sense of collective empowerment within communities. When individuals within a community believe in themselves and their capacity to create positive change, they come together to tackle societal challenges, drive progress, and make their community a better place for all.

As we navigate the complex and interconnected world of the 21st century, the belief in our abilities takes on greater significance. It is not only a personal force for transformation but also a societal and global force for positive change. When individuals, communities, and nations collectively believe in their abilities, they can address the most pressing global challenges, from climate change to social inequality.

In conclusion, belief in our abilities is a force that transcends the individual and radiates outward, influencing the world in profound ways. It is a catalyst for personal growth, resilience, and achievement. Moreover, it is a beacon of inspiration that empowers others to believe in themselves and create positive change in their lives and communities. As you embrace and nurture your own belief in your abilities, remember the ripple effect it can have on the world, and let it guide you toward a future filled with limitless possibilities for yourself and for all those you touch along the way.

In the grand tapestry of life, success often hinges on more than just talent and circumstance. It's about having the right mindset, a mindset that can inspire momentum and propel us towards our goals. The way we perceive and approach life's challenges can make all the difference in our journey.

Our mindset is the lens through which we view the world. A growth mindset, one that embraces challenges and sees failures as opportunities for growth, is a powerful catalyst for momentum. When we believe that our abilities and intelligence can be developed through dedication and hard work, we become more resilient in the face of setbacks. This resilience drives us forward, helping us overcome obstacles and keep going when the going gets tough.

Positive thinking is another crucial aspect of the mindset that inspires momentum. It's not about ignoring problems or being unrealistic; rather, it's about focusing on solutions and opportunities. A positive mindset encourages us to see the silver lining, even in the darkest of clouds. When we maintain a positive outlook, we become more open to creative solutions, and our enthusiasm can be infectious, rallying those around us to join in the pursuit of our goals.

Moreover, mindfulness plays a vital role in fostering the right mindset. Being present in the moment, appreciating the journey, and practicing gratitude can help us stay grounded and motivated. Mindfulness allows us to break free from the shackles of anxiety about the future or regrets about the past. It keeps our attention on what we can control now, thus propelling us forward with greater purpose and focus.

The company we keep also influences our mindset and, consequently, our momentum in life. Surrounding ourselves with positive, supportive individuals who share our goals can provide the encouragement and accountability we need. These connections can inspire us to push our boundaries, learn from others' experiences, and maintain our forward momentum.

Adopting a growth mindset, embracing positivity, practicing mindfulness, and nurturing a supportive community are all critical components of cultivating the right mindset to inspire momentum in life. When we approach life with these principles in mind, we become unstoppable forces of progress, capable of achieving our dreams and aspirations. So, let us remember that the power to ignite momentum lies within us, in our minds, waiting to be harnessed and directed toward a brighter future.

In addition to these core elements of mindset, setting clear goals and maintaining a sense of purpose are essential for sustaining momentum. Goals act as guiding stars, providing direction and focus to our efforts. When we know what we want to achieve, it becomes easier to channel our energy and resources toward those objectives. Furthermore, having a sense of purpose gives our actions a deeper meaning. It infuses our endeavors with passion and determination, making us more willing to endure the challenges that arise on our path.

A key factor in maintaining momentum is resilience. Life is rarely a smooth journey, and setbacks are inevitable. However, a resilient mindset allows us to bounce back stronger from failures and setbacks. Instead of being discouraged, we see these experiences as opportunities to learn, adapt, and grow. This resilience enables us to keep moving forward, even when faced with adversity.

It's also important to recognize the role of self-belief in inspiring momentum. Believing in our abilities and trusting our judgment is a powerful motivator. When we have confidence in ourselves, we are more willing to take risks and step out of our comfort zones. This willingness to take calculated risks often leads to new opportunities and breakthroughs that propel us further along our journey.

The journey to success is not always linear. There will be moments of doubt and uncertainty, but it's during these times that our mindset becomes a beacon of hope. It reminds us of our potential, our strengths, and our capacity for growth. It encourages us to persist, adapt, and keep moving forward, no matter the obstacles in our way.

The proper mindset is a formidable force that can inspire momentum in life. It encompasses a growth mindset, positivity, mindfulness, a supportive community, clear goals, purpose, resilience, self-belief, and adaptability. With this mindset, we become unstoppable in our pursuit of success, and even the most challenging circumstances become opportunities for growth. So, let us nurture and cultivate our mindset, for it is the driving force that can turn our dreams into reality and propel us toward a brighter future.

The power of the mind extends far beyond our immediate thoughts and emotions; it holds sway over virtually every aspect of our lives. Our mindset, thoughts, and beliefs serve as the control center for our actions, decisions, and ultimately, our destiny.

First and foremost, our mind shapes our perception of reality. It filters and interprets the world around us based on our beliefs and past experiences. Two people can experience the same event, yet their reactions may differ significantly because of their individual mindsets. This perception of reality directly influences our emotions, as how we perceive events and situations can trigger specific emotional responses.

Furthermore, our thoughts are the blueprint for our actions. When we have a clear and positive mindset, our thoughts tend to be constructive and solution-oriented. Conversely, a negative or defeatist mindset can lead to self-doubt and inaction. It's often said that "whether you think you can or you think you can't, you're right." This statement underscores the profound influence our thoughts have on our ability to achieve our goals.

Our mindset also dictates our decision-making. The choices we make in life are guided by our beliefs, values, and priorities, all of which are products of our mental conditioning. A person with a growth mindset might take on challenges and pursue learning opportunities, while someone with a fixed mindset might shy away from challenges and stick to what they know. Our decisions have a ripple effect on our lives, shaping our trajectory and impacting our overall well-being.

Furthermore, our mind controls our behaviors and habits. Habits, whether positive or negative, are formed through repeated actions driven by our thoughts and desires. A person who cultivates a disciplined and focused mindset is more likely to develop productive habits, such as regular exercise, healthy eating, and consistent work routines. On the other hand, a negative or undisciplined mindset can lead to destructive habits that hinder personal growth.

Our mind's influence extends to our relationships as well. The way we perceive ourselves, our self-esteem, and our self-worth all influence the quality of our interactions with others. Positive self-perception can lead to healthier relationships, while negative self-perception can create barriers to intimacy and connection.

Beyond our personal lives, our collective mindset as a society shapes our culture, institutions, and even the course of history. Social movements, political ideologies, and cultural norms are all products of collective mindsets. The collective mindset can either foster progress and positive change or perpetuate harmful biases and inequalities.

In essence, our mind is the commander-in-chief of our lives. It influences our perception, emotions, decisions, actions, habits, relationships, and even our impact on the world. Recognizing the immense power of the mind underscores the importance of cultivating a mindset that aligns with our goals and values, one that inspires positive momentum and leads us toward a fulfilling and purposeful life.

Moreover, the mind's control over life extends to our physical health. The field of psychosomatic medicine has shown that our mental and emotional state can have a direct impact on our physical well-being. Stress, for example, is a mental state that can lead to a range of physical ailments, from cardiovascular issues to digestive problems. Conversely, a positive and relaxed mindset can promote better physical health by reducing stress levels and enhancing the body's ability to heal itself.

Our mind also plays a critical role in setting and achieving long-term goals. When we set clear, well-defined goals and maintain a determined mindset, we create a roadmap for our future. This roadmap guides our daily actions, ensuring that they align with our aspirations. It's the mind's ability to envision a brighter future and break it down into actionable steps that enables us to make progress and achieve our dreams.

Additionally, our mind has the power to shape our beliefs and attitudes toward success and failure. Those who view setbacks as valuable learning experiences are more likely to persevere and ultimately succeed. On the other hand, those who dwell on failures and setbacks may become demotivated and abandon their pursuits prematurely. Our mindset can be the determining factor in whether we bounce back from failures or allow them to derail our progress.

Furthermore, the mind can influence our creativity and innovation. A mindset that encourages curiosity and open-mindedness can lead to groundbreaking discoveries and novel solutions to complex problems. Creative geniuses throughout history have harnessed the power of their minds to reshape entire industries and societies.

In essence, the mind serves as the master conductor of our life's symphony. It orchestrates our thoughts, emotions, actions, and decisions, shaping our destiny in profound ways. The mind's control over life is both a tremendous responsibility and an incredible opportunity. By nurturing a positive, growth-oriented mindset, we can unlock our full potential and create a life filled with purpose, achievement, and fulfillment.

The mind is not merely an observer of life but a creator and controller of it. It influences every facet of our existence, from our perception of reality to our physical health, from our relationships to our achievements. Understanding and harnessing the power of the mind is the key to unlocking the full potential of our lives. It is through our mindset that we can inspire momentum, overcome challenges, and shape a future that aligns with our aspirations and values.

Furthermore, our mind's influence on life extends to our overall well-being and happiness. Research in the field of positive psychology has shown that our mindset can greatly affect our sense of fulfillment and contentment. Those who cultivate a positive and grateful mindset tend to experience higher levels of happiness and life satisfaction. This is because a positive mindset allows us to appreciate the present moment, savor small joys, and find meaning in our experiences, leading to a more fulfilling life.

The mind also governs our perception of time. How we perceive time can profoundly impact our decisions and actions. A forward-thinking mindset, which focuses on long-term goals and delayed gratification, can lead to more prudent financial choices, healthier lifestyle habits, and greater personal growth. Conversely, a present-focused mindset that prioritizes immediate pleasures can lead to impulsive decisions and hinder our long-term progress.

Our mind even plays a role in shaping our physical environment. Innovations and inventions often begin as ideas in the minds of creative individuals. From art and architecture to technology and science, the mind's ability to conceive and design has shaped the world we live in today. The buildings we inhabit, the devices we use, and the systems that govern our societies all started as mental constructs.

Additionally, our mind has the power to influence our resilience in the face of adversity. A mindset that embraces challenges as opportunities for growth can help us navigate difficult times with grace and determination. It enables us to see setbacks as temporary and setbacks as opportunities to learn and improve. This resilience can be a powerful force in overcoming obstacles and maintaining momentum in life.

The mind's control over life is pervasive and profound. It shapes our perception, emotions, decisions, actions, relationships, health, goals, creativity, happiness, and even our physical environment. Recognizing the immense influence of the mind underscores the importance of actively cultivating a mindset that aligns with our values and aspirations. By doing so, we can harness the incredible power of the mind to inspire momentum, lead a purposeful life, and shape a better world for ourselves and those around us.

In the grand theater of life, the stage is set not by external circumstances alone but by the script written within our minds. Our mindset, the lens through which we perceive and interact with the world, has an unparalleled impact on every facet of our existence. It is the key that unlocks our potential, shapes our experiences, and defines our journey. In this long-form post, we will explore the profound influence of the proper mindset on all aspects of life.

Mindset Shapes Our Reality

Our mindset serves as the architect of our reality. It filters and interprets the events and situations we encounter, coloring them with our beliefs and emotions. Two individuals facing the same challenge may experience entirely different realities based on their mindsets. A positive and growth-oriented mindset allows us to see opportunities in difficulties, while a negative and fixed mindset can lead to a sense of helplessness.

Consider the power of optimism. A mindset that leans towards optimism can transform adversity into a chance for growth. It allows us to find silver linings, seek solutions, and remain resilient in the face of setbacks. This mindset shift can ultimately lead to more favorable outcomes, as it changes how we approach and respond to challenges.

Mindset Drives Our Behavior

Our mindset shapes our thoughts, which, in turn, influence our actions. When we possess a clear and focused mindset, our thoughts become the blueprint for our behavior. A growth mindset encourages us to pursue challenges and embrace learning opportunities, fostering personal and professional development. In contrast, a fixed mindset can stifle growth, as it leads to self-doubt and the avoidance of challenges.

The impact of mindset on behavior extends to our habits. Our daily routines and habits are the result of repeated actions driven by our thoughts and desires. A disciplined and determined mindset can lead to the development of positive habits such as regular exercise, healthy eating, and consistent work habits. On the other hand, a negative or undisciplined mindset can give rise to destructive habits that hinder personal growth.

Mindset Influences Decision-Making

The choices we make in life are profoundly influenced by our mindset. Our beliefs, values, and priorities—all products of our mental conditioning—guide our decision-making process. A person with a growth-oriented mindset may be more inclined to take calculated risks and explore uncharted territories, while someone with a fixed mindset may opt for safety and familiarity.

Moreover, our mindset dictates our approach to long-term goals. When we have a clear sense of purpose and maintain a determined mindset, we create a roadmap for our future. This roadmap shapes our daily decisions, ensuring they align with our aspirations. It's the mind's ability to envision a brighter future and break it down into actionable steps that enables us to make progress and achieve our dreams.

Mindset Shapes Relationships

Our mindset significantly impacts our relationships with others. How we perceive ourselves, our self-esteem, and our self-worth are all influenced by our mindset. A positive self-perception can lead to healthier relationships, as it fosters confidence and open communication. Conversely, a negative self-perception can create barriers to intimacy and connection.

Furthermore, our mindset affects our interactions with others. A mindset that values empathy, understanding, and cooperation can lead to more harmonious relationships. On the other hand, a mindset characterized by negativity, judgment, or defensiveness can lead to conflicts and strained connections.

Mindset and Physical Well-Being

The mind-body connection is well-established in fields like psychosomatic medicine. Our mental and emotional state can have a direct impact on our physical health. For instance, chronic stress, which stems from a negative mindset, can lead to a range of health issues, including cardiovascular problems, digestive disorders, and weakened immune function.

Conversely, a positive and relaxed mindset can promote better physical health by reducing stress levels and enhancing the body's ability to heal itself. Practices like mindfulness and stress management are rooted in the belief that nurturing a positive mindset can lead to improved physical well-being.

Mindset Shapes Time Perception

Our mindset can profoundly affect our perception of time and our orientation toward the past, present, and future. A forward-thinking mindset emphasizes long-term goals, delayed gratification, and investment in future outcomes. This orientation can lead to more prudent financial choices, healthier lifestyle habits, and greater personal growth.

Conversely, a present-focused mindset that prioritizes immediate pleasures and instant gratification can lead to impulsive decisions that hinder long-term progress. Understanding the role of mindset in time perception can help individuals make more informed choices and allocate their resources wisely.

Mindset Fosters Resilience

The way we view setbacks and failures is heavily influenced by our mindset. Those who maintain a growth-oriented mindset tend to view setbacks as valuable learning experiences. They see failure not as a dead-end but as a stepping stone toward success. This perspective fosters resilience, as it enables individuals to bounce back stronger from setbacks.

In contrast, a fixed mindset can lead to discouragement and self-doubt in the face of failure. Such individuals may be more prone to giving up prematurely, as they perceive setbacks as proof of their limitations. The resilience nurtured by a positive mindset allows individuals to endure challenges, maintain momentum, and continue progressing toward their goals.

Mindset Fuels Creativity and Innovation

Creativity and innovation often spring from a mindset that values curiosity, open-mindedness, and the willingness to explore the unknown. When we maintain a mindset that encourages these qualities, we become more receptive to new ideas and unconventional solutions. This mindset fosters an environment where groundbreaking discoveries and novel solutions can emerge.

Throughout history, creative geniuses have harnessed the power of their minds to reshape entire industries and societies. Innovations that have revolutionized the world, from the printing press to the internet, were born in the minds of individuals who dared to think differently and embrace a mindset of exploration and innovation.

Mindset Shapes Societal Impact

On a broader scale, our collective mindset as a society shapes our culture, institutions, and even the course of history. Social movements, political ideologies, and cultural norms are all products of collective mindsets. These mindsets can either foster progress and positive change or perpetuate harmful biases and inequalities.

Societal mindsets have the power to shape policies, influence public opinion, and drive collective action. Movements for civil rights, environmental conservation, and gender equality are all examples of how collective mindsets can lead to transformative societal changes. Recognizing the role of mindset in shaping the world underscores the importance of fostering positive, inclusive, and forward-thinking collective mindsets.

The Journey to Cultivating the Proper Mindset

Cultivating the proper mindset is not a one-time endeavor but an ongoing journey. It involves self-awareness, introspection, and a commitment to personal growth. Here are some key principles to consider on the path to developing a mindset that positively impacts all aspects of life:

Self-Awareness: Begin by examining your current mindset. Are there areas where you tend to have a fixed mindset? What limiting beliefs do you hold? Self-awareness is the first step in initiating change.

Embrace Growth: Adopt a growth mindset by believing in your capacity for learning and improvement. Embrace challenges as opportunities to grow and learn, rather than as threats to your abilities.

Cultivate Positivity: Practice positivity by focusing on solutions and opportunities rather than dwelling on problems. Cultivate gratitude and optimism to shape your emotional responses.

Practice Mindfulness: Incorporate mindfulness into your daily life. Mindfulness helps you stay present, appreciate the journey, and manage stress. It allows you to break free from anxiety about the future or regrets about the past, keeping your attention on what you can control in the present moment.

Set Clear Goals: Define your goals and aspirations clearly. A well-defined goal gives you a sense of direction and purpose. Break down larger goals into smaller, actionable steps that align with your long-term vision.

Maintain Resilience: Cultivate resilience by reframing setbacks as opportunities for growth. Embrace failures as stepping stones to success, and don't let them deter you from your path.

Build Self-Belief: Develop self-belief in your abilities and judgment. Trust yourself to make decisions and take calculated risks. Confidence in yourself can propel you to take action and pursue your goals with determination.

Surround Yourself with Support: Build a supportive network of friends, family, mentors, and like-minded individuals who share your goals and values. Surrounding yourself with positive and supportive people can provide encouragement, motivation, and accountability.

Reflect and Adjust: Regularly reflect on your mindset and its impact on your life. Are there areas where you need to make adjustments? Be open to refining your mindset as you learn and grow.

Practice Self-Compassion: Be kind to yourself along the journey. Understand that developing the proper mindset is a process, and there will be setbacks. Treat yourself with the same compassion you extend to others.

The proper mindset is a formidable force that can influence every aspect of our lives. It shapes our perception of reality, guides our behavior, influences our decision-making, impacts our relationships, and even plays a role in our physical well-being. Our mindset affects how we perceive time, our resilience in the face of adversity, our creativity, and innovation, and even our societal impact.

Recognizing the profound influence of mindset underscores the importance of actively cultivating and nurturing a mindset that aligns with our goals, values, and aspirations. It is through our mindset that we can inspire momentum, overcome challenges, and shape a future that reflects our vision of a fulfilling and purposeful life. The journey to developing the proper mindset is ongoing, but it is a journey that can lead to personal transformation and a positive impact on the world around us.

Breaking Free from Limiting Beliefs: How Negativity Impacts Our Lives

Negativity, with its insidious ability to infiltrate our thoughts and beliefs, can cast a shadow over our lives and hinder our potential. It manifests in the form of limiting beliefs and thoughts, creating self-imposed barriers that hold us back from reaching our full potential. In this long-form post, we will delve into the profound impact of negativity on our lives and explore strategies to break free from the constraints of limiting beliefs.

The Power of Limiting Beliefs

Limiting beliefs are those deeply ingrained thoughts and convictions that constrain our actions and decisions. They often stem from negative experiences, societal conditioning, or self-doubt. While these beliefs may seem innocuous, they can have a profound impact on our lives by shaping our perceptions and dictating our choices.

One common limiting belief is the fear of failure. Many people avoid taking risks or pursuing their dreams because they fear the potential for failure. This fear can paralyze individuals, preventing them from seizing opportunities that could lead to personal or professional growth.

Another common limiting belief is the idea of not being "good enough." Whether it's in the context of relationships, career, or personal pursuits, this belief can erode self-esteem and prevent individuals from pursuing their goals with confidence.

Negativity often finds a home in our self-talk—the ongoing internal dialogue we have with ourselves. Negative self-talk is a corrosive force that reinforces limiting beliefs and perpetuates a cycle of self-doubt. Phrases like "I can't," "I'm not capable," or "I'll never succeed" become self-fulfilling prophecies when repeated often enough.

For example, someone with a limiting belief related to their abilities might constantly tell themselves, "I'm not good at public speaking." As a result, they avoid public speaking opportunities, missing out on chances to improve their skills and boost their self-confidence.

Limiting beliefs and negative thoughts can significantly influence our decision-making. When we believe we are incapable or unworthy, we may choose to play it safe rather than take risks. This cautious approach can hinder personal growth and limit our opportunities for success.

For instance, someone with a limiting belief about their ability to start a business might shy away from entrepreneurial ventures, even if they have a great business idea. This fear-driven decision can lead to regret and missed opportunities.

Negativity doesn't just affect our professional lives; it can seep into our relationships and impact our self-worth. A negative self-image can make it challenging to form healthy, fulfilling connections with others. It can lead to feelings of inadequacy, insecurity, and a constant need for validation.

Furthermore, negativity can affect our ability to set boundaries and advocate for our needs in relationships. We may tolerate unhealthy dynamics or settle for less than we deserve due to a belief that we don't deserve better.

Recognizing the pervasive influence of negativity on our lives is the first step toward breaking free from its grip. Here are some strategies to challenge and overcome limiting beliefs and negative thoughts:

Start by identifying the limiting beliefs and negative self-talk patterns in your life. Pay attention to the thoughts and phrases that hold you back.

Once you've identified a limiting belief, question its validity. Ask yourself if there is evidence to support or refute it. Often, you'll find that these beliefs are based on assumptions rather than facts.

When negative thoughts arise, consciously replace them with more positive and empowering alternatives. For example, if you catch yourself thinking, "I'm not good enough," replace it with "I am capable, and I can learn and grow."

Share your struggles with trusted friends, family members, or a therapist. They can provide encouragement, perspective, and guidance as you work to overcome limiting beliefs.

Start with achievable, incremental goals that challenge your limiting beliefs. As you experience success, your confidence will grow, and your beliefs will begin to shift.

Be kind to yourself throughout this process. Understand that everyone has limiting beliefs, and it's part of the human experience to work through them.

Use visualization techniques to imagine yourself succeeding in areas where you have limiting beliefs. Visualization can help rewire your brain and build confidence.

Create positive affirmations that counteract your limiting beliefs. Repeat these affirmations regularly to reinforce positive self-talk.

As we work to challenge and overcome limiting beliefs and negative thoughts, we open ourselves up to a world of possibilities. Positivity, with its ability to instill confidence, resilience, and a growth mindset, can transform our lives in remarkable ways.

Consider the story of someone who once believed they were not good enough for a particular career. By challenging that limiting belief, seeking support, and setting small goals, they may ultimately find success and fulfillment in their chosen field. The shift from negativity to positivity can lead to a profound change in their life trajectory.

A growth mindset is a powerful antidote to limiting beliefs and negativity. This mindset acknowledges that abilities and intelligence can be developed through dedication and hard work. It encourages learning, resilience, and the belief that setbacks are opportunities for growth.

By cultivating a growth mindset, we can approach life's challenges with greater confidence and enthusiasm. We become more willing to take risks, embrace new opportunities, and persevere in the face of setbacks. This mindset shift not only empowers us to break free from limiting beliefs but also inspires personal and professional growth.

Negativity, in the form of limiting beliefs and negative thoughts, has the potential to cast a long shadow over our lives. However, with self-awareness, determination, and a commitment to positivity, we can break free from its constraints. By challenging and redefining our beliefs, fostering a growth mindset, and practicing self-compassion, we open the door to a life transformed by positivity.

Remember that the journey to overcoming negativity is ongoing, and setbacks may occur along the way. However, with each step forward, you gain greater control over your thoughts and beliefs, empowering yourself to live a life guided by confidence, resilience, and a belief in your own potential. As you embrace positivity, you'll find that the limitations of the past no longer define your future, and a world of opportunities awaits.

In the midst of the global COVID-19 pandemic, where countless individuals faced financial uncertainty and hardship, there emerged a remarkable story of resilience and transformation. This is the story of John, a man who, against all odds, overcame financial adversity through the power of the Law of Attraction.

At the onset of the pandemic, John, like many others, found himself facing unforeseen challenges. He had lost his job, and with bills piling up and a family to support, the future looked bleak. It was during this time of uncertainty that John stumbled upon the concept of the Law of Attraction, a belief that positive thoughts and intentions can manifest into reality.

With nothing left to lose, he decided to put this concept to the test.

John began each day with a ritual of gratitude. Despite the dire circumstances, he focused on the things he was thankful for—a loving family, good health, and the opportunity for personal growth. He visualized a better future, vividly imagining himself in a fulfilling job, providing for his family, and achieving financial stability. Instead of dwelling on his current hardships, he shifted his mindset to one of abundance and possibility.

As days turned into weeks, John's newfound positive mindset started to yield unexpected results. He began networking, connecting with professionals in his field, and pursuing job opportunities with renewed confidence. He approached each interview with a sense of conviction, believing that the right opportunity would come his way. And it did.

A few months into his journey, John received a job offer that not only matched his skillset but exceeded his expectations. It was as if the universe had conspired to reward his newfound optimism and determination. With a steady income once again, John began to pay off his debts and rebuild his financial stability.

But John's story didn't end there. As he continued to apply the Law of Attraction principles to his life, he noticed a series of unexpected windfalls. From a surprise bonus at work to a chance encounter that led to a side business opportunity, his life seemed to be filled with serendipitous moments.

As the pandemic slowly receded, John's financial situation continued to improve. He had not only secured a stable job but had also launched a successful side venture that brought in additional income. The Law of Attraction had become an integral part of his life, guiding him toward abundance, opportunities, and a newfound sense of purpose.

John's story serves as a testament to the power of the Law of Attraction, even in the face of daunting challenges. It demonstrates that by shifting one's mindset from scarcity to abundance, and by unwaveringly believing in the possibility of a brighter future, remarkable transformations can occur. In a time when many were grappling with uncertainty, John's journey serves as an inspiring reminder that the power of positive thinking can indeed manifest profound change, even during the darkest of times.

Once upon a time in a quaint little town, there lived a woman named Emma. Emma had weathered the storms of life, including a painful divorce that left her feeling broken and disillusioned about love. She had spent years in a loveless marriage, and after her divorce, she questioned whether she could ever find true love again. However, Emma was determined to turn her life around and believed in the power of the Law of Attraction and positive thinking.

Emma's journey began with self-reflection. She realized that to attract love into her life, she first needed to cultivate love within herself. She started a journal of daily affirmations, filling its pages with declarations of self-love, worthiness, and optimism. Each morning, she looked in the mirror and repeated these affirmations, slowly but surely mending her self-esteem that had been shattered by her failed marriage.

One sunny morning, as Emma was strolling through a local park, she noticed a colorful poster for a community yoga class. Intrigued by the idea of holistic healing, she decided to give it a try. Yoga became her sanctuary, a place where she found inner peace and balance. She met like-minded individuals who radiated positivity and self-acceptance, and it was there that she discovered the importance of self-care and mindfulness.

Emma's newfound self-love was a beacon of positivity that attracted the attention of others. Friends and acquaintances began to notice her vibrant energy and the joy she exuded. She started attending social gatherings and community events, not with the sole purpose of finding love, but to connect with others and build meaningful relationships.

One evening, at a local art exhibition, Emma's eyes met those of a kind-hearted artist named Daniel. He was drawn to her magnetic aura, and they struck up a conversation about their shared passion for art and self-discovery. Daniel was a man who appreciated the beauty in life and saw the world through a lens of creativity and wonder.

As Emma and Daniel spent more time together, their connection deepened. They found solace in each other's company, sharing their dreams, fears, and aspirations. Emma's positive outlook on life was a balm to Daniel's soul, and he admired her resilience in the face of adversity.

One starry night, under a canopy of twinkling stars, Daniel confessed his feelings to Emma. He told her that he had never met anyone like her, someone who radiated such positivity and self-assuredness. Emma, with tears of joy in her eyes, realized that she had attracted love into her life through her unwavering belief in the power of the Law of Attraction and the transformational force of positive thinking.

Their love blossomed like a beautiful garden in spring, vibrant and full of life. Emma and Daniel's relationship was built on a foundation of mutual respect, trust, and a shared journey of self-discovery. They embarked on adventures together, explored new horizons, and continued to grow both individually and as a couple.

Emma's story serves as a testament to the transformative power of the Law of Attraction and positive thinking. Through her journey of self-love and personal growth, she not only attracted love into her life but also found a partner who cherished her for the radiant and resilient woman she had become. In the embrace of this newfound love, Emma realized that the path to happiness begins within, and with the right mindset and a heart open to possibilities, love can bloom even after the darkest of storms.

As Emma and Daniel's love story continued to unfold, it was clear that their connection was something truly special. They supported each other's passions and dreams, encouraging one another to pursue their deepest desires. Emma's positive outlook on life continued to be a guiding light for both of them, reminding them that they could conquer any challenge together.

One sunny afternoon, while taking a leisurely walk in the park, Daniel surprised Emma with a small, beautifully wrapped gift. As she opened it, she discovered a journal with a heartfelt note inside. The note read, "For the woman who has inspired me to see the world with new eyes and to believe in the power of love and positivity." It was a journal for them to document their journey together, filled with memories, dreams, and affirmations of their love.

Emma and Daniel's relationship deepened with each passing day. They learned to communicate openly, resolving any challenges that arose with grace and understanding. Emma's journey of self-love had not only attracted a loving partner but had also given her the tools to nurture a healthy and thriving relationship.

As their love story continued, Emma and Daniel decided to blend their lives further. They moved in together, creating a harmonious space that reflected their shared values and dreams. Emma's vision board, adorned with images of love, adventure, and a bright future, hung prominently in their home as a daily reminder of their intentions.

One beautiful evening, while sitting together under a blanket of stars, Daniel took Emma's hand and whispered, "I am so grateful to have you in my life. You've shown me the incredible power of positivity and the beauty of believing in the Law of Attraction." Emma smiled warmly, knowing that their love had been not just a stroke of luck but a manifestation of their combined optimism and faith in the universe.

Their love story was a testament to the idea that love can be found and nurtured at any stage in life, even after the darkest of times. Emma had transformed her life through the power of positive thinking and self-love, and in doing so, she had attracted a love that was deep, meaningful, and built on a foundation of shared values and genuine affection.

As they continued their journey together, Emma and Daniel knew that life would bring its challenges, but they also believed that their love and positivity would help them overcome any obstacle. Their love story was a testament to the idea that, no matter the past, the power of the heart and the mind could shape a beautiful and fulfilling future. Emma had found not only love but a partner who shared her belief in the transformative power of a positive mindset, making their journey together all the more magical.

In the intricate tapestry of life, the most potent thread weaving together the fabric of our reality is not external circumstances, but rather the state of our own minds. It is a profound and universal truth that our mindset holds the key to shaping the world we experience. The thoughts we harbor, the beliefs we hold, and the attitudes we nurture wield an unparalleled influence over our perception of reality and, by extension, the course of our lives.

Consider for a moment the concept that reality is subjective. The same event, viewed through different mindsets, can yield strikingly different interpretations. A setback, for instance, may be seen as a devastating failure to one person and as a valuable learning experience to another. Our mindset acts as a lens through which we filter and make sense of the world, and it has the remarkable power to transform ordinary events into extraordinary opportunities.

Moreover, our mindset shapes our emotional landscape. The emotions we experience are direct products of our thoughts and beliefs. When we adopt a mindset of gratitude, we tend to find joy and contentment in the simplest of moments. Conversely, a negative or pessimistic mindset can cast a shadow over even the most fortunate circumstances. The emotional tapestry of our lives is intricately woven with the threads of our thoughts, making our mindset the chief architect of our emotional reality.

Our mindset also wields tremendous influence over our actions and behaviors. When we maintain a positive and determined mindset, our thoughts are imbued with a sense of possibility and purpose. We are more likely to take risks, set ambitious goals, and persist in the face of adversity. In contrast, a defeatist or self-limiting mindset can stifle initiative, preventing us from seizing opportunities and realizing our potential. The choices we make, the paths we choose, and the actions we take are all guided by the compass of our mindset.

Furthermore, our mindset shapes the way we interact with others and navigate our relationships. The self-image we hold influences our self-esteem and self-worth, impacting the quality of our interactions. A mindset rooted in self-acceptance and confidence tends to foster healthier, more fulfilling relationships. On the other hand, a mindset plagued by self-doubt and insecurity can create barriers to intimacy and connection. Our perception of others and our ability to empathize are likewise influenced by our mindset, as it determines whether we approach people with openness or suspicion.

The impact of mindset extends beyond the individual to the collective. Societal beliefs, values, and attitudes are formed by the collective mindsets of its members. Social movements, cultural norms, and political ideologies are all products of shared mindsets. The course of history itself is shaped by the collective beliefs and actions of societies. Consider the transformative power of collective mindsets, such as those behind civil rights movements, environmental conservation efforts, or movements for gender equality. These movements have demonstrated the capacity of like-minded individuals to effect profound change on a global scale.

In essence, our mindset is not merely a passive observer of reality but an active shaper of it. It is the force that sculpts our perception, emotions, actions, and interactions. It is the silent hand that molds the clay of our lives, giving form to our experiences and determining the paths we tread. Recognizing the profound influence of mindset underscores the significance of actively cultivating and nurturing a mindset that aligns with our values and aspirations. It is through our mindset that we determine whether we see the world as a place of abundance or scarcity, opportunity or obstacle, joy or despair.

The most valuable realization one can embrace is that their mindset is the master key that unlocks the door to their reality. It is the cornerstone upon which their life is built. By acknowledging the immense power of the mind, individuals hold the key to transforming their world. They can choose to cultivate a mindset that fosters positivity, resilience, and growth, leading to a life rich with possibilities and purpose. In the grand tapestry of existence, the mindset is the brush that paints the colors of reality, and by wielding it consciously, individuals can create a masterpiece of their own design.

Within the realm of mindset, the importance of self-talk stands as a cornerstone. Self-talk is the intimate conversation we hold with ourselves, the ongoing dialogue that shapes our thoughts and beliefs. It is the internal narrative that can either empower or undermine us. Understanding and harnessing the power of self-talk is a fundamental aspect of cultivating a mindset that determines our reality.

Consider self-talk as the storyteller of our lives. The stories we tell ourselves, the interpretations we give to events, and the judgments we pass on our actions are all part of this inner narrative. Positive self-talk can be a powerful ally, as it narrates stories of resilience, growth, and self-empowerment. It reinforces the belief that challenges are opportunities, mistakes are lessons, and that we possess the strength to overcome adversity.

Conversely, negative self-talk can be a relentless antagonist, perpetuating stories of self-doubt, limitation, and inadequacy. It crafts a narrative where setbacks are insurmountable, abilities are fixed, and success is beyond reach. Such self-talk can become a self-fulfilling prophecy, as it influences our decisions, actions, and the outcomes we ultimately experience.

Self-talk is not only about the stories we tell but also about the tone and language we use. The words we choose to describe ourselves and our experiences have a profound impact on our emotions and self-image. Harsh self-criticism, self-blame, and negative labels can erode self-esteem and self-worth. Conversely, self-compassion, encouragement, and positive affirmations can nurture a sense of self-acceptance and self-belief.

The significance of self-talk becomes particularly pronounced during challenging times. When faced with adversity, our internal dialogue can determine whether we perceive difficulties as insurmountable obstacles or as opportunities for growth. Those who engage in constructive self-talk view setbacks as stepping stones to success, whereas those mired in negative self-talk may perceive the same setbacks as failures.

Furthermore, self-talk plays a pivotal role in shaping our emotions. The thoughts we entertain in our minds directly influence our emotional state. When we engage in positive self-talk, we can invoke feelings of optimism, hope, and resilience even in the face of adversity. In contrast, negative self-talk can trigger emotions like anxiety, self-doubt, and despair.

Self-talk also significantly affects our decision-making. The internal narrative we hold guides our choices, as we tend to align our actions with our beliefs. Positive self-talk can inspire us to take risks, pursue goals, and persevere through challenges. It instills the belief that we have the capacity to learn, adapt, and overcome obstacles. On the other hand, negative self-talk can lead to self-imposed limitations, hesitation, and a reluctance to step outside our comfort zones.

Recognizing the importance of self-talk highlights the need to cultivate a mindful and empowering inner dialogue. It involves monitoring our thoughts and challenging self-limiting beliefs. When negative self-talk arises, we can consciously reframe it, replacing it with more positive and constructive alternatives.

Practicing self-compassion is another essential aspect of nurturing a healthy self-talk. Treating ourselves with the same kindness and understanding that we offer to others can transform our inner narrative from one of criticism to one of support and encouragement.

Moreover, incorporating positive affirmations into our daily routine can be a powerful tool for reshaping self-talk. These affirmations serve as statements of intention and belief, reinforcing a positive mindset and nurturing self-confidence.

And self-talk is the storyteller of our lives and the narrator of our reality. It molds our thoughts, beliefs, emotions, actions, and, ultimately, our experiences. The narratives we choose to embrace within our minds wield immense power, determining whether we perceive life as an adventure filled with possibilities or as a series of insurmountable challenges. Cultivating a positive and empowering self-talk is not only an essential component of a growth-oriented mindset but also a transformative force that can lead to a reality defined by resilience, self-belief, and the pursuit of one's fullest potential.

Furthermore, the relationship between self-talk and our overall well-being cannot be overstated. Studies have shown that individuals who engage in positive self-talk tend to experience lower levels of stress and anxiety. By countering negative thoughts with constructive and affirming self-talk, we can reduce the mental and emotional burdens that often accompany life's challenges.

Self-talk also plays a pivotal role in building resilience. When we face setbacks or adversities, a positive inner dialogue can serve as a source of inner strength. It reminds us of our past successes and reinforces our ability to overcome obstacles. This resilience, in turn, empowers us to bounce back from adversity with newfound determination.

Moreover, self-talk impacts our physical well-being. The mind and body are intimately connected, and the thoughts we harbor can influence our physical health. Positive self-talk can boost the immune system, lower blood pressure, and promote overall well-being. On the other hand, chronic negative self-talk has been associated with increased stress-related illnesses and a compromised immune response.

The beauty of self-talk is that it is a skill that can be cultivated and refined over time. It requires self-awareness, practice, and a commitment to nurturing a mindset that serves our well-being and aspirations. It is not about denying the existence of challenges or glossing over difficulties but about reframing our perspective and adopting a constructive and solution-oriented approach.

To harness the power of self-talk effectively, consider the following strategies:

Start by becoming aware of your inner dialogue. Pay attention to the thoughts and beliefs that regularly arise in your mind.

When you identify negative or self-limiting thoughts, question their validity. Ask yourself if there is evidence to support or refute them. Often, negative thoughts are based on assumptions rather than facts.

Replace negative self-talk with more positive and empowering alternatives. For example, if you catch yourself thinking, "I can't do this," replace it with "I am capable, and I can learn and grow."

Create positive affirmations that counteract your limiting beliefs. Repeat these affirmations regularly to reinforce positive self-talk.

Treat yourself with kindness and understanding. Understand that everyone has moments of self-doubt, and it's part of the human experience to work through them.

Share your self-talk challenges with trusted friends, family members, or a therapist. They can provide encouragement, perspective, and guidance as you work to improve your self-talk.

Keep a journal to track your thoughts and emotions. This can help you identify patterns in your self-talk and track your progress in cultivating a more positive mindset.

So self-talk is the bridge between the inner world of our thoughts and beliefs and the external reality we experience. It shapes our perception, emotions, actions, and overall well-being. By recognizing its profound influence and actively cultivating a positive and empowering inner dialogue, we not only enhance our mindset but also transform our reality. Self-talk is a potent tool for navigating life's challenges, fostering resilience, and ultimately crafting a reality defined by optimism, self-belief, and the pursuit of our fullest potential. It is a reminder that, in the grand narrative of our lives, we are the authors of our own stories, and the words we choose to write have the power to shape a reality filled with possibility and purpose.

In the vast and mysterious realm of human potential, there exists a concept that has captured the imagination of countless individuals: the Law of Attraction. It is a belief that the thoughts and intentions we hold in our minds have the power to shape our reality, attracting into our lives the experiences, people, and circumstances that align with our innermost desires. At the heart of this transformative principle lies the undeniable power of the human mind, a force that can be harnessed to manifest our dreams and aspirations into tangible existence.

The Law of Attraction: A Brief Overview

The Law of Attraction posits that like attracts like, meaning that the energy and vibrations we emit through our thoughts and feelings draw similar energies and experiences into our lives. It operates on the premise that the universe is an interconnected web of energy, and our thoughts are the threads that weave our destinies within this intricate tapestry.

To understand the power of the mind in the Law of Attraction, we must first acknowledge the profound interplay between our thoughts, emotions, and actions.

Thoughts: The Blueprint of Our Reality

Our thoughts are the architects of our reality. They lay the foundation upon which the Law of Attraction operates. When we think about what we desire—whether it's success, love, abundance, or happiness—we set in motion a series of events and energies that align with those desires. Our thoughts act as a blueprint for the universe, guiding the creative process of manifestation.

Emotions: The Fuel of Manifestation

While thoughts are the blueprint, emotions serve as the fuel that propels our desires into reality. The intensity of our emotions amplifies the vibrational frequency of our thoughts. When we feel a deep sense of joy, gratitude, or passion in connection with our desires, we emit a powerful energetic signal that resonates with similar frequencies in the universe.

Conversely, negative emotions, such as fear, doubt, or anxiety, can act as obstacles to manifestation. They send conflicting signals to the universe, causing resistance and hindering the attraction of our desires. Therefore, mastering our emotional landscape is a crucial aspect of harnessing the Law of Attraction.

Actions: The Bridge Between Thought and Reality

Thoughts and emotions alone are not enough to bring our desires into fruition. They must be coupled with inspired action. Action is the bridge that connects our inner world of thoughts and feelings with the external world of tangible results. The Law of Attraction does not promote a passive approach to life but encourages proactive steps toward our goals.

When we align our actions with our intentions, we create a harmonious synergy between our internal and external worlds. Action serves as a tangible declaration of our commitment to our desires and reinforces the belief that our dreams are within reach.

The Power of Visualization and Affirmations

Two powerful techniques that illustrate the mind's influence in the Law of Attraction are visualization and affirmations.

Visualization involves vividly imagining the realization of our desires. By mentally experiencing the sensations, emotions, and details associated with our goals, we enhance our belief in their attainability. Visualization harnesses the mind's creative power, aligning it with the universe's energy to manifest our desires.

Affirmations are positive statements that reinforce our beliefs and intentions. Repeated regularly, affirmations can reprogram our subconscious mind, replacing limiting beliefs with empowering ones. They serve as reminders of our potential and align our thoughts with our desires.

Overcoming Limiting Beliefs

To fully harness the power of the mind in the Law of Attraction, we must confront and overcome limiting beliefs. These are deeply ingrained thought patterns that undermine our confidence and self-worth. Limiting beliefs act as roadblocks to manifestation, sabotaging our efforts by emitting contradictory vibrations.

The process of shedding limiting beliefs involves self-awareness, self-compassion, and conscious effort to reframe negative thought patterns. As we replace self-doubt with self-belief, we open the gateway to unlimited potential.

Patience and Trust

It is important to note that the Law of Attraction is not a magic wand that instantly transforms our lives. It requires patience, trust, and unwavering belief in the process. The universe operates on its own timeline, and our role is to maintain faith in our desires and consistently align our thoughts, emotions, and actions with them.

Unleashing the Power Within

In the grand tapestry of existence, the power of the mind in the Law of Attraction is a profound and transformative force. It empowers individuals to shape their destinies, manifest their dreams, and create a reality that aligns with their deepest desires. By mastering their thoughts, emotions, and actions, individuals can become co-creators of their lives, harnessing the universal energies to bring their aspirations to life.

The journey of harnessing the power of the mind in the Law of Attraction is an exploration of the self, a discovery of one's potential, and a testament to the limitless capabilities of the human mind. It is an invitation to dream boldly, believe unwaveringly, and manifest magnificently. The power lies within, waiting to be awakened, harnessed, and unleashed, paving the way to a reality where dreams are transformed into living, breathing truths.

In the intricate web of human existence, where the mind and the universe dance in synchrony, there exists a profound realm that transcends the boundaries of the material world. This is the domain of spirituality, a sacred space where the human soul connects with a higher, universal consciousness. It is within this spiritual dimension that the Law of Attraction takes on a deeper, more profound significance—a bridge between the individual and the cosmos, where intentions and vibrations resonate in harmony with the universe's energies. In this long-form post, we will explore the transformative power of spirituality in the Law of Attraction and how the union of these forces can reshape the course of our lives.

The Spiritual Essence of the Law of Attraction

At its core, the Law of Attraction is founded on the principle that our thoughts and intentions have the power to shape our reality. When we align our internal desires with the vibrations of the universe, we begin to manifest our intentions into tangible existence. Spirituality infuses this process with a profound sense of purpose and connection. It acknowledges that we are not isolated beings but integral parts of a vast, interconnected cosmos.

The Role of Belief and Faith

In the spiritual dimension of the Law of Attraction, belief and faith play pivotal roles. Spirituality encourages individuals to embrace a deep-seated belief in the interconnectedness of all things and the existence of a higher intelligence or universal energy. This belief acts as a driving force, reinforcing the conviction that the universe is conspiring to fulfill our intentions.

Faith, in this context, is not limited to religious beliefs but extends to trust in the process of manifestation itself. It involves surrendering to the wisdom of the universe and believing that our intentions will manifest at the right time and in the right way. Faith is the unwavering assurance that our desires are heard and will be answered.

Meditation: The Gateway to Alignment

Meditation, a cornerstone of many spiritual practices, serves as a powerful tool for aligning with the energies of the Law of Attraction. It offers a pathway to inner peace, heightened awareness, and a deep connection with the universe. Through meditation, individuals can quiet the chatter of the mind, allowing them to access the stillness within, where intentions can be planted like seeds in fertile soil.

During meditation, individuals can visualize their desires and imbue them with positive emotions. This heightened state of consciousness enhances the vibrational frequency of their intentions, making them more aligned with the universal energies. As a result, the process of manifestation becomes more potent and effective.

Gratitude and the Law of Reciprocity

Spirituality emphasizes the practice of gratitude as a means of aligning with the Law of Attraction. Gratitude is a powerful force that not only uplifts the spirit but also magnetizes positive experiences into our lives. When we express gratitude for what we have, we signal to the universe that we are open to receiving more abundance and blessings.

The Law of Reciprocity, a spiritual principle, suggests that the universe responds to our actions and intentions in kind. When we give, whether it's love, kindness, or gratitude, the universe responds by giving back to us. By cultivating gratitude, we create a cycle of positive energy that attracts more of what we appreciate.

Detachment and Surrender

One of the paradoxes of the Law of Attraction within a spiritual context is the importance of detachment and surrender. While we set clear intentions and visualize our desires, we must also release our attachment to specific outcomes. This is where spirituality teaches the profound wisdom of surrendering to the divine order of the universe.

Detachment is not synonymous with indifference but rather an acknowledgment that there may be a higher purpose or plan beyond our comprehension. Surrendering our desires to the universe allows us to let go of anxiety and fear, opening the door for the universe to work its magic in ways that may surpass our limited human understanding.

The Ripple Effect: Serving Others

Spirituality in the Law of Attraction transcends the idea of personal gain and extends to the concept of service to others. Many spiritual teachings emphasize that true abundance is not measured solely by material wealth but by the positive impact we have on others and the world.

By aligning our intentions with the well-being and happiness of others, we activate the Law of Attraction in a way that benefits not only ourselves but also the collective consciousness. This ripple effect amplifies the vibrational frequencies of our intentions, attracting experiences and opportunities that contribute to the greater good.

A Holistic Approach to Manifestation

In conclusion, the power of spirituality in the Law of Attraction offers a holistic and transformative approach to manifestation. It invites individuals to transcend the limitations of the ego and connect with a higher, universal consciousness. Through belief, faith, meditation, gratitude, detachment, and service to others, spirituality enhances the vibrational frequencies of intentions, making them more aligned with the energies of the universe.

Ultimately, the union of spirituality and the Law of Attraction represents a harmonious dance between the individual and the cosmos—a partnership that empowers individuals to manifest their desires in alignment with

In the hustle and bustle of modern life, finding moments of stillness and reflection is essential for regaining focus, rekindling motivation, and building momentum towards our goals. Meditation is a powerful practice that can help us center ourselves, tap into our inner wisdom, and harness the energy needed to propel us forward. Here are 100 meditations designed to inspire and guide you on your journey to building momentum in life.

Mindset and Clarity

Morning Affirmations: Start your day with positive affirmations to set the tone for success.

Visualization: Picture your goals and dreams as vividly as possible.

Clearing the Mind: Let go of cluttered thoughts to create mental space.

The Power of Intentions: Reflect on your intentions for the day.

Inner Strength: Connect with your inner reservoir of strength and resilience.

Gratitude: Focus on the things you're grateful for to cultivate a positive mindset.

Future Self Meditation: Visualize your future self who has achieved your goals.

Letting Go of Limiting Beliefs: Release self-doubt and limiting beliefs.

The Growth Mindset: Embrace a mindset of growth and possibility.

Daily Mantra: Repeat a mantra that aligns with your aspirations.

Self-Love and Acceptance: Cultivate love and acceptance for yourself.

Forgiveness: Let go of resentment and forgive yourself and others.

Setting Clear Intentions: Clarify your goals and intentions for the day.

Mindful Breathing: Focus on your breath to center your mind.

Affirming Abundance: Affirm your abundance and attract prosperity.

Embracing Change: Meditate on the beauty and growth potential of change.

Overcoming Obstacles: Reflect on your ability to overcome challenges.

Morning Motivation: Gather energy and motivation for the day ahead.

Surrendering Control: Release the need for control and surrender to the flow of life.

Creating Balance: Visualize a balanced life where all your needs are met.

Goal Setting and Planning

Goal Clarity: Meditate on the clarity of your goals.

Daily Planning: Plan your day with intention and focus.

Breaking Barriers: Explore the steps to overcome obstacles.

Visualization of Success: See yourself achieving your goals with joy.

Future Vision: Create a mental picture of your ideal future.

Inspired Action: Connect with the motivation to take action.

Eliminating Distractions: Release distractions from your mind.

Aligning with Purpose: Connect with your life's purpose.

Setting Priorities: Identify your top priorities for the day.

Focusing on What Matters: Meditate on what truly matters to you.

Energy and Productivity: Boost your energy for a productive day.

Overcoming Procrastination: Reflect on strategies to beat procrastination.

Visualization of Achievements: Picture your accomplishments.

Mindful Decision-Making: Approach decisions with mindfulness.

Inspired Ideas: Open your mind to creative and innovative ideas.

Morning Reflection: Reflect on your goals and intentions.

Daily Affirmation for Success: Affirm your commitment to success.

Inspiration from Within: Seek inspiration from your inner wisdom.

Gratitude for Progress: Express gratitude for your progress so far.

Alignment with Values: Ensure your actions align with your core values.

Resilience and Adversity

Inner Resilience: Connect with your inner strength and resilience.

Bouncing Back from Failure: Meditate on bouncing back stronger after setbacks.

Endurance and Perseverance: Cultivate endurance in the face of challenges.

Embracing Uncertainty: Find peace in the midst of uncertainty.

Releasing Anxiety: Let go of anxiety and stress.

Cultivating Patience: Foster patience as you work towards your goals.

Adapting to Change: Embrace change as a natural part of life.

Overcoming Fear: Conquer fear and step into courage.

Building Confidence: Strengthen your self-confidence.

Inner Peace and Serenity: Connect with your inner peace.

Detaching from Outcomes: Release attachment to specific outcomes.

Staying Positive in Challenges: Maintain a positive mindset during adversity.

Resilience Visualization: Picture yourself resilient in the face of challenges.

Overcoming Limiting Beliefs: Challenge and replace limiting beliefs.

Inner Compass: Tune into your inner guidance.

Embracing Setbacks as Growth: View setbacks as opportunities for growth.

Cultivating Hope: Nurture hope even in difficult circumstances.

Finding Light in Darkness: Seek positivity in challenging times.

Embracing Imperfection: Accept imperfection and embrace growth.

Inner Calm in Chaos: Find calmness within chaos.

Relationships and Connection

Loving-Kindness Meditation: Send love and kindness to yourself and others.

Empathy and Compassion: Cultivate empathy and compassion in your heart.

Relationship Harmony: Meditate on harmonious relationships.

Forgiveness and Healing: Send forgiveness and healing to those you've had conflicts with.

Attracting Positive Relationships: Focus on attracting positive people into your life.

Strengthening Connections: Strengthen your bonds with loved ones.

Communication and Understanding: Meditate on clear and understanding communication.

Embracing Differences: Accept and appreciate differences in others.

Conflict Resolution: Seek inner guidance for resolving conflicts peacefully.

Connecting with Humanity: Feel a deep connection with all living beings.

Self-Love and Healthy Relationships: Ensure self-love in relationships.

Appreciating Relationships: Express gratitude for the people in your life.

Serving Others with Love: Meditate on serving others with love and compassion.

Boundaries and Self-Care: Establish healthy boundaries in relationships.

Building Trust: Reflect on building trust in relationships.

Harmony with Nature: Connect with the natural world and its rhythms.

Love and Joy in Daily Interactions: Infuse love and joy into your interactions.

Positive Energy in Relationships: Radiate positive energy in your connections.

Building Community: Visualize a thriving, supportive community.

Family Harmony: Meditate on harmony within your family.

Health and Well-Being

Body Appreciation: Connect with gratitude and love for your body.

Healing Energy: Visualize healing energy flowing through your body.

Mindful Eating: Practice mindful eating for nourishment and balance.

Stress Reduction: Release stress and tension from your body.

Energizing Meditation: Boost your energy and vitality.

Immune System Boost: Strengthen your immune system with positive energy.

Restful Sleep: Prepare your mind for restful and rejuvenating sleep.

Balancing Hormones: Visualize hormonal balance in your body.

Pain Relief Meditation: Focus on pain relief and healing.

Relaxation and Renewal: Find deep relaxation and renewal.

Body-Mind Connection: Connect with the mind's influence on physical health.

Breathing for Calm: Practice deep breathing for relaxation.

Release of Tension: Let go of physical and emotional tension.

Healthy Habits: Visualize yourself adopting healthy habits effortlessly.

Vibrant Energy Flow: Meditate on the flow of vibrant energy within.

Joyful Movement: Embrace joyful movement and exercise.

Emotional Balance: Balance your emotions for overall well-being.

Inner Radiance: Connect with your inner radiance and vitality.

Restoring Energy: Recharge your energy and vitality.

Holistic Wellness: Meditate on holistic well-being in all aspects of life.

These 100 meditations are a treasure trove of tools for building momentum in life. By integrating them into your daily routine, you can tap into your inner potential, find clarity, and cultivate the resilience needed to achieve your goals. Remember that consistency is key, and as you embark on your meditation journey, you'll discover the transformative power of these practices in shaping a life filled with purpose, passion, and momentum.

Personally, for me, leaving behind a dead-end job I loathed was one of the most transformative decisions of my life. The thought of spending another day in that mundane office, chained to a desk with no sense of purpose, had become unbearable. It was as if the walls of my cubicle were closing in on me, and I knew I had to break free from the cycle of monotony. Little did I know that this leap of faith would lead me down an incredible path to becoming a multi-million dollar bestselling author, sharing the secrets of the Law of Attraction with eager audiences at seminars and conferences worldwide.

The turning point in my life came when I stumbled upon the Law of Attraction. It was like a beacon of hope amidst the darkness of my corporate existence. The idea that our thoughts and beliefs could shape our reality resonated deeply with me. I devoured books, attended workshops, and immersed myself in the world of manifestation. With each passing day, my passion for this subject grew stronger, and I knew I had found my calling.

Leaving my job was not an easy decision. The stability of a regular paycheck had its allure, but I realized that my true potential would never be unlocked within the confines of that office. So, with a heart full of dreams and a determination to succeed, I took the leap. It was a leap into the unknown, a leap fueled by a burning desire to share the magic of the Law of Attraction with the world.

The initial months were far from glamorous. Rejection letters from publishers piled up, and I struggled to make ends meet. But I refused to give in to self-doubt. I poured my heart and soul into writing, crafting a book that would become the cornerstone of my career. And then, it happened. My book was published, and it struck a chord with readers worldwide. It soared to the top of bestseller lists, and the royalties started pouring in.

As my book gained popularity, invitations to speak at seminars and conferences began to flood my inbox. It was a surreal feeling to stand before a crowd of eager faces, sharing the principles that had transformed my life. I saw firsthand how the Law of Attraction was changing the lives of those who embraced it. The energy in those rooms was electrifying, and I knew I was on the right path.

Over the years, my journey continued to unfold. I authored more books, each one building upon the foundation of the Law of Attraction. My seminars and conferences grew in scale and reach. The revenue generated from book sales and speaking engagements surpassed my wildest dreams. I was not just making a living; I was thriving, and I was helping others do the same.

Becoming a multi-million dollar bestselling author teaching the Law of Attraction was not just about financial success; it was about fulfilling my purpose. I had broken free from the shackles of a dead-end job I despised and had found my true calling. Today, I look back on that pivotal decision to leave the corporate world with gratitude. It was a leap of faith that allowed me to manifest a life beyond my wildest imagination, and I am honored to continue sharing the incredible power of the Law of Attraction with the world.

As I embarked on this incredible journey, I learned that success was not just about financial gains but about personal growth and transformation. Leaving my old job had forced me to confront my fears and doubts, pushing me to evolve into a stronger, more confident version of myself. I had to develop unwavering self-belief to weather the storms of rejection and uncertainty.

My career as a bestselling author and Law of Attraction teacher also opened doors to amazing opportunities I could never have imagined. I had the privilege of meeting and collaborating with like-minded individuals who shared my passion for personal development and spiritual growth. Together, we created life-changing programs and resources that touched the lives of countless people seeking positive change.

But perhaps the most rewarding aspect of my new life was the impact I had on others. The messages and emails I received from readers and seminar attendees were heartwarming. People shared stories of how the Law of Attraction had transformed their relationships, their health, and their financial situations. Knowing that I had played a part in helping them achieve their dreams was a source of immense satisfaction.

One of the most memorable moments of my career was when I received an invitation to speak at a prestigious international conference. I stood on a stage before thousands of people from different corners of the world, and I realized the profound reach of my message. The Law of Attraction was not limited by borders or boundaries; it was a universal principle that resonated with people from all walks of life.

Financially, my journey had taken me to a place of abundance beyond my wildest dreams. I was able to enjoy a lifestyle that included travel, luxury, and the freedom to pursue my passions without financial constraints. Yet, what truly fulfilled me was the knowledge that I was helping others find their own paths to prosperity and happiness.

Looking back, I couldn't help but marvel at the serendipity of it all. Leaving a job I hated had been a leap of faith, but it was a leap that propelled me toward a life of purpose, abundance, and fulfillment. It was a reminder that sometimes, the most significant transformations in life occur when we summon the courage to let go of what no longer serves us and embrace the unknown.

My journey from a dead-end job to becoming a multi-million dollar bestselling author and Law of Attraction teacher has been an incredible adventure. It has been a testament to the power of belief, determination, and the courage to pursue one's true calling. I am grateful every day for the opportunity to inspire and uplift others on their own paths to success and happiness, and I look forward to the exciting chapters that await in this remarkable journey of life.

The path I had chosen was not without its challenges, and there were moments of doubt along the way. However, those challenges only served to strengthen my resolve and deepen my understanding of the Law of Attraction. I learned that setbacks were simply opportunities for growth and that persistence was the key to manifesting my desires.

One of the most significant lessons I learned was the importance of mindset. The Law of Attraction isn't just about wishing for things to happen; it's about aligning your thoughts, beliefs, and actions with your desires. I had to continually work on my own mindset, shedding limiting beliefs and replacing them with empowering ones. It was a journey of self-discovery and self-improvement that mirrored the transformations I was guiding others through.

I also discovered the incredible power of gratitude. As I achieved greater success, I made it a practice to express gratitude for everything in my life. Gratitude amplified the positive energy I was putting out into the universe and attracted even more abundance and blessings. It was a beautiful cycle that reaffirmed the principles I was teaching.

Over the years, I expanded my reach through various media channels. I started a podcast, launched online courses, and even appeared on television and in documentaries discussing the Law of Attraction. The more I shared my knowledge, the more I saw lives change for the better. It was a fulfilling and humbling experience to witness the profound impact of these teachings on individuals and communities.

One of the highlights of my journey was the creation of a foundation dedicated to helping underprivileged individuals gain access to personal development resources. I firmly believed that everyone should have the opportunity to learn about the Law of Attraction and unlock their potential. Through the foundation's initiatives, we were able to reach people who had never before encountered these transformative principles.

As the years went by, my success as a bestselling author and Law of Attraction teacher continued to grow. I had the privilege of traveling the world, meeting extraordinary people, and experiencing the richness of different cultures. Along the way, I remained grounded in the understanding that the Law of Attraction was not a magic wand but a powerful tool that required dedication and inner work.

My journey from a dead-end job to becoming a multi-million dollar bestselling author teaching the Law of Attraction in seminars and conferences has been a remarkable adventure filled with personal growth, transformation, and a deep sense of purpose. It has been a testament to the incredible power of belief, mindset, and gratitude. I am grateful for the opportunity to inspire and empower others on their own paths of self-discovery and manifestation. And as I continue on this extraordinary journey, I am excited to see how the Law of Attraction will continue to shape not only my life but the lives of countless others who dare to dream and believe in the limitless possibilities of the universe.

The ongoing journey of sharing the Law of Attraction and helping others manifest their desires has led me to explore new horizons and expand my own understanding of the principles involved. I've had the privilege of collaborating with experts from various fields, including psychology, neuroscience, and spirituality. These collaborations have enriched my teachings and allowed me to provide a more comprehensive approach to personal development and manifestation.

One of the key insights I've gained is the importance of inner alignment. It's not enough to simply wish for external changes; true transformation begins within. Teaching individuals how to connect with their inner selves, identify their core desires, and release any emotional blocks has become an integral part of my seminars and courses. Witnessing participants undergo profound shifts in their lives has been incredibly rewarding.

In addition to speaking engagements and writing, I've embraced the digital age to reach an even broader audience. Social media platforms, webinars, and online communities have allowed me to connect with individuals from every corner of the globe. It's astonishing to think that the Law of Attraction has the power to unite people regardless of geographical boundaries, language barriers, or cultural differences.

Through these digital channels, I've also had the pleasure of interacting with a vibrant community of individuals who share their success stories, challenges, and breakthroughs. This sense of connection and the knowledge that we are all on this journey together has created a sense of purpose and fulfillment that goes beyond financial success.

While financial abundance has certainly been a part of my journey, I've come to understand that true wealth extends far beyond monetary gains. It encompasses a deep sense of fulfillment, a profound connection with others, and a life lived in alignment with one's values and passions. It's about living a life of purpose, where every day feels like a gift, and every interaction is an opportunity to inspire and uplift.

As I continue on this incredible path, I am reminded of the importance of staying humble and open-minded. The Law of Attraction is a vast and ever-expanding field, and there is always more to learn and discover. I remain committed to my own growth and evolution, knowing that my journey is far from over and that there are limitless possibilities waiting to be explored.

My journey from a dead-end job to becoming a multi-million dollar bestselling author teaching the Law of Attraction in seminars and conferences has been a profound and transformative adventure. It has been a journey of self-discovery, personal growth, and the joy of helping others unlock their potential. I am deeply grateful for the opportunities I've been given and for the incredible individuals I've had the privilege to meet along the way. As I look to the future, I am excited to see how the Law of Attraction will continue to shape and enrich not only my life but the lives of countless others who choose to embrace its principles and create their own extraordinary destinies.

I want to share a powerful truth with you—one that has the potential to change your life in ways you may not have imagined. It's a simple yet profound concept that has been echoed by countless success stories throughout history: You can accomplish anything you set your mind to if you persevere.

At times, life can be challenging. We all face obstacles, setbacks, and moments of self-doubt. It's easy to feel overwhelmed and believe that our goals and dreams are out of reach. But I'm here to tell you that those obstacles are not insurmountable, and your dreams are not unattainable.

The key to achieving your aspirations lies in your unwavering determination and perseverance. It's about setting a clear vision, setting small, achievable goals along the way, and staying committed to your journey, no matter how tough it may get. Here are a few reasons why perseverance is your greatest ally:

Resilience in the Face of Challenges: Challenges are a natural part of life's journey. They test our resolve, but they also provide opportunities for growth. Perseverance means facing adversity head-on and not allowing it to deter you from your path. Each obstacle you overcome brings you one step closer to your goal.

Learning and Adaptation: Along your journey, you'll acquire valuable knowledge and experience. You'll learn from your mistakes and refine your approach. Perseverance allows you to adapt, adjust, and keep moving forward, armed with the lessons learned from your setbacks.

Building Character: The process of persevering builds character and resilience. It instills in you qualities like patience, determination, and grit—qualities that not only help you achieve your goals but also make you a stronger, more capable individual.

Inspiration to Others: Your journey of perseverance can inspire others around you. When they witness your determination and witness your progress, they may be inspired to pursue their own dreams and goals, creating a ripple effect of positive change.

Achieving the Unthinkable: Perseverance has led individuals to achieve what many considered impossible. Think of inventors who faced countless failures before creating groundbreaking inventions or athletes who trained relentlessly to reach the pinnacle of their sport. Their stories are a testament to the power of unwavering determination.

Remember that success is not always measured by the speed at which you reach your goals, but by the fact that you never gave up on them. It's not about comparing yourself to others; it's about becoming the best version of yourself.

As you embark on your journey, keep your vision clear, stay focused on your goals, and never underestimate the power of perseverance. The road may be challenging, but with each step you take, you are inching closer to your dreams.

Believe in yourself, trust the process, and know that you have the capacity to accomplish anything you set your mind to.

So, my dear reader, embrace perseverance as your guiding light. Let it be the force that propels you forward, no matter how daunting the path may seem. Your dreams are within reach, and with unwavering determination, you can make them a reality. It's time to take that first step and begin your journey towards the extraordinary life you deserve.

Continuing on the path of perseverance, let's explore some practical steps and mindset shifts that can help you harness this incredible force to achieve your dreams:

1. Define Your Goals: The first step in any journey is to have a clear destination. What do you want to accomplish? Define your goals with specificity. Whether it's starting a new career,

launching a business, getting fit, or mastering a skill, knowing exactly what you want is crucial.

2. Break It Down: Big goals can feel overwhelming. To make them manageable, break them down into smaller, actionable steps. These bite-sized tasks become milestones on your journey, making the path forward more achievable.

3. Create a Plan: A well-thought-out plan is your roadmap to success. It's not enough to have goals; you need a strategy to reach them. Set deadlines, allocate resources, and create a timeline for your journey.

4. Stay Consistent: Consistency is the bedrock of perseverance. Make a commitment to work on your goals regularly, even when motivation wanes. Remember, it's the daily grind that leads to extraordinary results.

5. Embrace Failure as Feedback: Understand that failure is not a sign of defeat but a stepping stone to success. Each setback is an opportunity to learn, grow, and refine your approach. Thomas Edison famously said, "I have not failed. I've just found 10,000 ways that won't work."

6. Cultivate Patience: Rome wasn't built in a day, and neither are most significant achievements. Patience is your ally in the face of slow progress. Trust that your efforts will compound over time, leading to significant results.

7. Surround Yourself with Support: Building a support network can provide encouragement and motivation during challenging times. Share your goals with trusted friends or mentors who can offer guidance and cheer you on.

8. Visualize Success: Spend time each day visualizing yourself achieving your goals. This

practice not only keeps your vision clear but also reinforces your belief in your abilities.

9. Celebrate Small Wins: Don't wait until you've reached the finish line to celebrate. Acknowledge and celebrate your small victories along the way. It boosts your confidence and keeps you motivated.

10. Adapt and Adjust: As you progress, you may encounter unexpected obstacles or changes in circumstances. Be flexible and willing to adjust your plan as needed while keeping your ultimate goal in mind.

11. Maintain Self-Belief: Self-doubt is a natural part of any journey, but it should never deter you. Remind yourself of your capabilities and the reasons you started in the first place. Surround yourself with positive affirmations and inspiring stories of others who have persevered.

12. Never Give Up: Finally, the most crucial piece of advice is never to give up. Perseverance means pushing through when things get tough, even when the road ahead seems impossible. Remember, the moment you feel like giving up could be the moment right before a breakthrough.

The power of perseverance is within your reach. It's the secret sauce that turns dreams into reality, transforms challenges into opportunities, and leads ordinary individuals to achieve extraordinary feats. As you embark on your journey towards your goals, carry these principles with you, and let them guide you towards the life you've always envisioned.

You have the strength, the determination, and the resilience to accomplish anything you set your mind to. Embrace perseverance as your constant companion, and watch as it propels you to heights you never thought possible.

In a world filled with distractions, challenges, and ever-increasing demands, the ability to self-motivate is nothing short of a superpower. Self-motivation, often referred to as intrinsic motivation, is the driving force that propels individuals to take action, pursue their goals, and achieve remarkable success. It is a critical element in personal development, professional growth, and overall happiness. In this post, we will delve deep into the importance of self-motivation and explore how you can harness this incredible force to transform your life.

1. Self-Motivation Fuels Ambition: At the core of self-motivation lies ambition—the burning desire to achieve something greater. Whether it's a career milestone, a fitness goal, or a creative endeavor, ambition is the spark that ignites action. Without self-motivation, ambitions remain dormant dreams, never given the chance to materialize.

2. Overcoming Procrastination: Procrastination is the arch-nemesis of progress. It lures us into the comforting embrace of inaction, preventing us from reaching our full potential. Self-motivation acts as a powerful antidote to procrastination, pushing us to start, continue, and complete tasks even when they seem daunting.

3. Resilience in the Face of Challenges: Life is filled with ups and downs, and it's easy to lose motivation when faced with setbacks. Self-motivated individuals possess the resilience to bounce back from disappointments, using failures as stepping stones rather than stumbling blocks. They understand that challenges are part of the journey, not roadblocks to success.

4. Independence and Autonomy: Relying solely on external motivation can be precarious. Self-motivated individuals, on the other hand, are self-reliant. They don't wait for external

validation or rewards to take action. Their motivation comes from within, giving them a sense of independence and autonomy over their choices and actions.

5. Continuous Self-Improvement: Self-motivation is closely tied to the pursuit of self-improvement. Those who are driven by intrinsic motivation are constantly seeking ways to learn, grow, and evolve. They understand that personal development is a lifelong journey, and they embrace it wholeheartedly.

6. Achieving Long-term Goals: Long-term goals often require sustained effort and dedication. Self-motivation provides the stamina needed to stay committed to those goals over extended periods. Whether it's building a successful business, completing a degree, or maintaining a healthy lifestyle, self-motivation keeps the momentum going.

7. Building Confidence: As you achieve goals and overcome challenges through self-motivation, your self-confidence naturally grows. Each accomplishment becomes a testament to your abilities, reinforcing the belief that you can achieve even more.

8. Cultivating a Positive Mindset: Self-motivated individuals tend to have a more positive outlook on life. They focus on solutions rather than problems, viewing setbacks as opportunities to learn and grow. This positive mindset not only drives motivation but also attracts positivity and opportunities into their lives.

9. Leading by Example: Self-motivated individuals often serve as role models for others. Their dedication and determination inspire those around them to strive for their own goals and tap into their inner motivation.

10. Fulfillment and Happiness: Ultimately, self-motivation leads to a deep sense of fulfillment and happiness. When you set meaningful goals and work tirelessly to achieve them, you experience a profound sense of purpose and contentment.

So, how can you cultivate and harness the power of self-motivation in your own life?

1. Identify Your Why: Understand the underlying reasons and values that drive your goals. Knowing why you want to achieve something will fuel your motivation.

2. Set Clear Goals: Define your goals with clarity, specificity, and deadlines. Break them down into smaller, manageable steps.

3. Create a Vision Board: Visual representation of your goals can serve as a powerful reminder of what you're working towards.

4. Develop Positive Habits: Cultivate habits that support your goals and motivate you to take consistent action.

5. Seek Inspiration: Surround yourself with inspiring books, quotes, and individuals who motivate you to stay on track.

6. Practice Self-Compassion: Be kind to yourself on your journey. Recognize that setbacks are normal, and self-compassion can rekindle your motivation.

7. Stay Accountable: Share your goals with a trusted friend or mentor who can hold you accountable for your progress.

In conclusion, self-motivation is the engine that drives personal and professional success. It is the inner fire that propels you forward, even in the face of challenges and uncertainties. By understanding its importance and actively cultivating it in your life, you can unlock your full potential and embark on a journey of continuous growth and achievement. Remember, the power to motivate yourself lies within you; all you need to do is ignite it.

The metaphysics of creation delves deep into the workings of the mind, exploring the profound connection between our thoughts, consciousness, and the manifestation of our reality. In this philosophical journey, we encounter the idea that the mind is not just a passive observer of the world but an active participant in the process of creation itself.

At its core, the metaphysics of creation posits that thoughts are not mere fleeting mental events but powerful forces that shape the fabric of our existence. The mind is seen as a creative engine, capable of generating ideas, beliefs, and intentions that influence the course of our lives. This concept echoes the ancient wisdom found in various spiritual and philosophical traditions, from the Law of Attraction to the teachings of Eastern philosophies like Buddhism and Taoism.

In this metaphysical framework, thoughts are not isolated occurrences but interconnected threads in a vast tapestry of consciousness. They are energy patterns that resonate with the vibrational frequencies of the universe. When we focus our thoughts and intentions on a particular outcome, we send out energetic signals that interact with the universal field of potentiality. This interaction sets in motion a process of creation, drawing to us the people, circumstances, and events that align with our mental vibrations.

The role of belief is paramount in the metaphysics of creation. Our beliefs serve as the foundation upon which our thoughts are built. They act as filters through which we perceive and interpret reality. If we hold limiting beliefs that constrain our possibilities, our thoughts will reflect those limitations, and our creations will be similarly restricted. Conversely, when we cultivate empowering beliefs that affirm our potential, our thoughts become powerful catalysts for positive change.

The mind's creative potential extends beyond the realm of individual desires. It is believed that collective consciousness also plays a pivotal role in shaping the world we inhabit. The collective thoughts, beliefs, and intentions of humanity generate a collective field of influence, affecting global events, social dynamics, and the overall state of the world. This perspective underscores the responsibility we each bear for the collective reality we co-create through our thoughts and actions.

The metaphysics of creation invites us to become conscious creators of our reality, recognizing that our thoughts have the power to shape our destiny. It challenges us to take responsibility for the quality of our inner world, understanding that our outer experiences are a reflection of our inner state. This philosophy empowers us to break free from victimhood and become active agents of change in our lives.

However, the metaphysics of creation is not a call to abandon reason and embrace wishful thinking. It emphasizes the importance of aligning our thoughts with our authentic desires and values. It encourages critical self-reflection, self-awareness, and mindfulness as tools for navigating the creative process consciously.

The metaphysics of creation offers a profound perspective on the workings of the mind and its role in shaping our reality. It challenges us to recognize the creative power of our thoughts, the influence of our beliefs, and the interconnectedness of consciousness in the grand tapestry of existence. It invites us to step into the role of conscious creators, empowering us to co-author the story of our lives and contribute to the evolution of human consciousness itself.

The metaphysics of creation also introduces the concept of intention as a key element in the process of manifestation. Intention goes beyond mere wishful thinking; it is a deliberate and focused desire, coupled with a strong belief in its realization. When we set clear intentions, we are directing the creative power of the mind toward a specific outcome. Intention acts as a guiding force, steering our thoughts, decisions, and actions toward the realization of our desires.

One of the intriguing aspects of this metaphysical perspective is the notion of synchronicity. Synchronicity is the occurrence of meaningful coincidences that seem to defy conventional explanations. In the metaphysics of creation, synchronicities are seen as signs and confirmations from the universe that we are in alignment with our desires. They serve as feedback loops, indicating that our thoughts and intentions are resonating with the greater intelligence of the cosmos.

Moreover, this philosophy underscores the interconnectedness of all life and the idea that we are not separate from the world we create. The mind is not isolated but exists in a dynamic relationship with the larger field of consciousness. This interconnectedness extends to our interactions with others, emphasizing the potential for co-creation and collaboration. When individuals come together with shared intentions, their collective creative power is amplified, leading to the emergence of shared realities and innovations.

It's essential to recognize that the metaphysics of creation is not a departure from science or reason but rather an expansion of our understanding of the mind and its role in shaping reality. It complements scientific principles such as quantum physics, which explore the fundamental nature of the universe, including the role of consciousness in the observation and manifestation of physical phenomena.

In practical terms, embracing the metaphysics of creation invites us to become more mindful of our thoughts and intentions. It encourages us to cultivate a positive and empowering inner dialogue, eliminate self-limiting beliefs, and set clear intentions for what we wish to create in our lives. It reminds us that we are co-creators of our reality, and by aligning our thoughts, beliefs, and intentions with our true desires, we have the power to bring about transformative change in our lives and in the world around us.

The metaphysics of creation offers a profound perspective on the mind's role in shaping our reality. It invites us to explore the interconnectedness of consciousness, the power of intention, and the significance of synchronicity in our lives. Embracing this philosophy empowers us to become conscious creators of our destiny, guiding us toward a more purposeful and fulfilling existence. It challenges us to step into our role as co-authors of the grand narrative of the universe, shaping our lives and the world with every thought, belief, and intention we hold.

The Road to Success: Why There Are No Shortcuts

In a world that often celebrates quick fixes, hacks, and instant gratification, it's crucial to remind ourselves that there arc no shortcuts to genuine, lasting success. True success is the result of hard work, perseverance, and a commitment to personal and professional growth. In this post, we will explore why shortcuts to success are an illusion and why the journey itself is just as important as the destination.

1. Mastery Takes Time: Whether you're striving for excellence in a skill, profession, or craft, true mastery requires time and dedication. Malcolm Gladwell's "10,000-hour rule" suggests that it takes roughly 10,000 hours of practice to achieve mastery in any field. This level of commitment cannot be circumvented by shortcuts.

2. Learning from Failure: Failure is an integral part of the journey to success. It provides valuable lessons, sharpens your skills, and builds resilience. Shortcuts often bypass these essential learning experiences, robbing you of the growth and wisdom that come from overcoming challenges.

3. Building a Strong Foundation: Success built on shortcuts is like a house of cards; it's fragile and unsustainable. A solid foundation is necessary to support lasting success. Taking the time to acquire knowledge, develop skills, and gain experience is akin to laying a strong foundation for your achievements.

4. Trust and Credibility: Trust is an essential element of success in any endeavor. Whether you're building a career, a business, or relationships, trust is cultivated over time through consistent actions and integrity. Shortcuts erode trust and credibility, which can be difficult to regain once lost.

5. Character Development: The journey to success is not just about external achievements but also about personal growth and character development. It's about becoming the kind of person who can handle success responsibly and

gracefully. Shortcuts can skip this crucial aspect of the journey.

6. Sustainable Success vs. Short-Term Gains: Shortcuts often lead to short-term gains or quick wins. Sustainable success, on the other hand, is built on a solid foundation and withstands the test of time. It's about achieving not just what you want but also what you need for long-term fulfillment.

7. Authenticity and Passion: Success is most rewarding when it aligns with your authentic self and passions. The journey to success allows you to discover your true purpose and values, helping you create a life that is deeply meaningful and fulfilling.

8. Appreciating the Process: Success is not solely about reaching a destination; it's also about appreciating the journey itself. The challenges, the growth, the setbacks, and the

small victories along the way contribute to a rich and fulfilling life.

9. Inspirational Role Models: Many successful individuals have faced adversity, setbacks, and long, arduous journeys. Their stories serve as inspiration, reminding us that success is achievable through hard work and perseverance.

10. Longevity and Legacy: Lasting success is often associated with a legacy that endures beyond one's lifetime. Shortcuts may yield temporary success, but they rarely leave a lasting impact or legacy that inspires future generations.

The road to success is a marathon, not a sprint. While shortcuts may offer the allure of quick rewards, they often lead to shallow and short-lived success. True success is about the journey, the growth, the lessons, and the enduring impact you make on the world. It's about striving for excellence, pursuing your passions, and becoming the best version of yourself. So, embrace the path of hard work, dedication, and perseverance, for it is on this journey that you will find the true essence of success—a journey worth taking and savoring every step of the way.

As we continue to explore the idea that there are no shortcuts to success, it's important to address some common misconceptions and pitfalls that can lead people astray when they seek quick and easy routes to achievement.

1. The Illusion of Overnight Success: In the age of social media and instant fame, it's easy to be deceived by stories of overnight success. However, these stories often omit the years of hard work, failures, and perseverance that preceded the breakthrough moment. True success is rarely instant; it is the result of consistent effort and dedication over time.

2. The Cost of Shortcuts: Shortcuts may provide temporary gains, but they often come at a cost.

They can lead to compromises in quality, ethical dilemmas, and long-term consequences that outweigh any immediate benefits. Success built on shortcuts is fragile and can crumble when exposed to scrutiny.

3. The Comparison Trap: Comparing your progress to others who appear to have taken shortcuts can be demoralizing and counterproductive. Remember that everyone's journey is unique, and success is not one-size-fits-all. Focus on your own path and what you can control.

4. Shortcuts vs. Efficiency: It's essential to differentiate between shortcuts and efficiency. Efficiency involves finding smarter, more effective ways to achieve your goals without compromising quality or integrity. Efficiency is a valuable skill, but it should not be confused with shortcuts that sacrifice essential elements of success.

5. Embracing the Learning Curve: Success often involves a learning curve, and shortcuts can bypass this valuable phase. Embracing the process of learning, growth, and skill development is an integral part of achieving meaningful success.

6. Shortcuts as a Last Resort: In some situations, shortcuts may be considered as a last resort when faced with a time-sensitive or critical decision. However, even in these cases, careful consideration of the potential consequences is crucial.

7. The Role of Persistence: Persistence is the bedrock of long-term success. It is the determination to keep going when faced with obstacles and setbacks. Shortcuts may provide a momentary escape from challenges, but they do not cultivate the resilience that true success demands.

In your pursuit of success, it's important to set realistic expectations and recognize that the journey will have its share of ups and downs. Success is not a linear path, and setbacks are an inevitable part of the process. Embrace the challenges and setbacks as opportunities for growth and learning, for they are often the stepping stones to eventual triumph.

Ultimately, the realization that there are no shortcuts to success can be liberating. It frees you from the pressure to achieve quick results and allows you to focus on the deeper, more meaningful aspects of your journey. It encourages you to invest in yourself, your skills, and your passions, knowing that true success is not a destination but a lifelong pursuit of excellence and fulfillment. So, embark on your journey with determination, and remember that it is in the enduring effort and unwavering commitment that you will find the genuine and lasting success you seek.

In the fast-paced world we live in, it's easy to become overwhelmed by the constant hustle and bustle of life. The demands of work, relationships, and the never-ending stream of information from the digital age can leave us feeling stressed, anxious, and disconnected from our inner selves. In the midst of this chaos, daily prayer and meditation stand as powerful tools to help us find peace, purpose, and a deeper connection to our spiritual essence.

Prayer is a practice that transcends cultures, religions, and beliefs. It is a way for individuals to communicate with a higher power, the universe, or their own inner wisdom. Daily prayer offers a sacred space for reflection, gratitude, and seeking guidance. Here are some compelling reasons why daily prayer is of paramount importance:

Gratitude and Positivity: Daily prayer encourages us to start our day with a heart full of gratitude. Expressing thanks for the simple blessings in life helps us shift our focus from what we lack to what we have, fostering a more positive mindset.

Connection to the Divine: For those who believe in a higher power, daily prayer is a means to connect with the divine. It is an opportunity to seek guidance, strength, and solace in times of need.

Stress Reduction: Engaging in daily prayer can be incredibly calming. It allows us to release stress and anxiety, promoting emotional well-being and mental clarity.

Self-Reflection: Through prayer, we can reflect on our actions, thoughts, and intentions. It provides a space for self-awareness and self-improvement.

Community and Belonging: Many religious communities emphasize the importance of daily prayer. It creates a sense of belonging and unity among members who come together in worship.

The Power of Daily Meditation

Meditation is the practice of training the mind to focus and redirect thoughts. While prayer often involves speaking or seeking answers, meditation is about listening, observing, and being present in the moment. Here's why daily meditation is crucial:

Mindfulness: Meditation is a powerful tool for cultivating mindfulness, the practice of being fully present in the moment. This can enhance our awareness of our thoughts, emotions, and surroundings.

Stress Reduction: Just like prayer, meditation is known for its stress-reducing benefits. Regular practice can lower cortisol levels, decrease anxiety, and promote relaxation.

Improved Concentration: Daily meditation enhances our ability to concentrate and sustain attention. It sharpens our mental faculties and can lead to better decision-making.

Emotional Regulation: Meditation helps us better understand and manage our emotions. It allows us to respond to situations with greater clarity and less reactivity.

Spiritual Growth: While meditation is often associated with Eastern spiritual traditions, it can also be a deeply spiritual experience for individuals of various beliefs. It can lead to profound insights and personal growth.

The true power of daily prayer and meditation lies in their synergy. When practiced together, they create a holistic approach to spiritual well-being and self-discovery. Prayer provides a means of communication with a higher power or the universe, while meditation facilitates inner peace, self-awareness, and personal growth.

To integrate these practices into your daily life, consider establishing a morning routine that includes both prayer and meditation. Find a quiet space, set aside dedicated time, and be consistent. There is no one-size-fits-all approach; your practice should align with your beliefs and preferences.

And so daily prayer and meditation are not just religious rituals; they are transformative practices that can enhance our physical, mental, and spiritual well-being. In the chaos of our modern lives, they serve as anchors, helping us find inner peace, purpose, and a deeper connection to ourselves and the world around us. Whether you seek solace, personal growth, or simply a moment of stillness, daily prayer and meditation offer profound and lasting benefits.

While the benefits of daily prayer and meditation have been appreciated for centuries, modern science has also delved into their profound effects on the human mind and body. Research has shown that these practices have a tangible impact on our overall well-being.

Neuroplasticity: Daily meditation has been found to increase the brain's neuroplasticity, which is the ability to form new neural connections. This can lead to enhanced cognitive functions, improved memory, and a sharper mind.

Stress Reduction: Scientific studies have consistently demonstrated the stress-reducing effects of both daily prayer and meditation. They can lower cortisol levels, reduce blood pressure, and mitigate the harmful effects of chronic stress.

Emotional Health: Meditation has been shown to increase gray matter density in brain regions associated with emotional regulation and self-control. This means that daily meditation can help individuals manage their emotions more effectively.

Pain Management: Meditation techniques have been incorporated into pain management programs. They can reduce the perception of pain and improve one's ability to cope with chronic pain conditions.

Enhanced Immunity: Daily prayer and meditation have been linked to improved immune function. A stronger immune system can help the body fend off illnesses and maintain overall health.

Better Sleep: Many individuals who practice meditation report improved sleep quality. Daily meditation can help calm racing thoughts and promote restful sleep.

Mind-Body Connection: These practices emphasize the interconnectedness of the mind and body. Regular meditation and prayer can lead to a better understanding of how mental and emotional states affect physical well-being.

The Role of Daily Prayer and Meditation in Self-Discovery

Beyond their physical and mental health benefits, daily prayer and meditation also play a crucial role in self-discovery and personal growth.

Self-Awareness: Daily meditation encourages self-awareness by inviting us to explore our inner thoughts and emotions without judgment. This heightened self-awareness can lead to greater self-acceptance and personal growth.

Empathy and Compassion: Prayer often involves seeking blessings and guidance not only for ourselves but also for others. This cultivates empathy and compassion, fostering a sense of interconnectedness with the world.

Spiritual Growth: For those on a spiritual journey, daily prayer and meditation can be transformative. They provide a path to deeper understanding, a sense of purpose, and a connection to something greater than ourselves.

Life Purpose: Through prayer and meditation, we can gain insights into our life's purpose and direction. It can help us clarify our values and priorities.

Resilience: These practices can build emotional resilience, helping us bounce back from adversity with grace and strength.

While the benefits of daily prayer and meditation are clear, establishing and maintaining a daily practice can be challenging. Life's demands often make it difficult to find the time and discipline required. However, the rewards are worth the effort.

To overcome challenges, start small. Dedicate just a few minutes each day to your practice and gradually increase the duration as it becomes a habit. Find a comfortable and quiet space, and consider using guided meditation apps or joining a prayer group for support and accountability.

So daily prayer and meditation are powerful tools for achieving a more balanced, peaceful, and purposeful life. They offer a way to navigate the complexities of the modern world while nurturing our spiritual selves. Whether for physical health, emotional well-being, or self-discovery, these practices hold a profound and enduring significance in our lives. By making them a daily ritual, we can tap into their transformative potential and experience the many benefits they have to offer.

While daily prayer and meditation can be deeply personal practices, they also have the power to foster a sense of community and connection among individuals. This sense of belonging can be as essential as the personal benefits they bring.

Group Prayer and Meditation: Many communities and religious groups come together to engage in daily prayer or meditation. This collective energy and shared intention can amplify the benefits and create a sense of unity among participants.

Support Network: Practicing daily prayer and meditation within a community or with loved ones can create a support network. Sharing your experiences, challenges, and breakthroughs with others can provide encouragement and a sense of camaraderie.

Cultural and Interfaith Exchange: Daily prayer and meditation are practiced in diverse ways across different cultures and faiths. Engaging in these practices can lead to a deeper understanding and appreciation of the world's rich tapestry of beliefs and traditions.

Moral and Ethical Guidance: For many, daily prayer provides a moral compass and a sense of ethical guidance. It helps individuals make decisions aligned with their values, promoting a more compassionate and just society.

In the digital age, we are bombarded with constant distractions, notifications, and the pressure to be constantly connected. Daily prayer and meditation offer a sanctuary of mindfulness amidst this digital chaos.

Digital Detox: Engaging in daily prayer and meditation allows us to detach from our screens and the online world. It's a time to disconnect from the external noise and reconnect with our inner selves.

Enhanced Focus: These practices train the mind to focus and concentrate, which can be particularly valuable in an age of information overload. The ability to stay present and focus on the task at hand becomes a valuable skill.

Reduced Stress: The constant barrage of information and the pressures of social media can lead to stress and anxiety. Daily prayer and meditation provide a respite, reducing stress levels and promoting emotional well-being.

Daily prayer and meditation are not quick fixes or one-time solutions. They are lifelong journeys that evolve and deepen over time. Just as our lives are constantly changing, so too will our experiences with these practices.

It's essential to approach daily prayer and meditation with patience and an open heart. There will be days when your mind is restless, and other days when you experience profound peace and clarity. The key is to continue, regardless of the fluctuations, knowing that these practices are guiding you on a path of self-discovery and growth.

In conclusion, the importance of daily prayer and meditation in our lives cannot be overstated. They offer a refuge from the chaos of the modern world, a pathway to self-discovery, and a means to nurture our spiritual and emotional well-being. By integrating these practices into our daily routines, we embark on a transformative journey that not only benefits ourselves but also ripples outward, touching the lives of those around us. Whether you seek inner peace, connection, or personal growth, daily prayer and meditation stand as timeless and invaluable tools on this profound journey of self-discovery and spiritual awakening.

Here are 50 affirmations for self-motivation to help you stay inspired and focused on your goals:

I am capable of achieving my dreams.

I am in control of my thoughts and actions.

Every challenge I face is an opportunity for growth.

I believe in my abilities to overcome obstacles.

I am resilient, and I bounce back from setbacks.

I am motivated to take action every day.

I am committed to my personal growth and success.

I attract positivity and abundance into my life.

I am constantly evolving and improving.

I trust in the timing of my life's journey.

I have the courage to pursue my passions.

I am worthy of success and happiness.

I am focused on my goals with unwavering determination.

I embrace change as a stepping stone to success.

I am disciplined and work diligently toward my goals.

I radiate confidence in everything I do.

I attract opportunities that align with my purpose.

I am the architect of my destiny.

I am resourceful and find solutions to challenges.

I am persistent and never give up on my dreams.

I am motivated by my inner fire and passion.

I am open to new experiences and opportunities.

I am worthy of love, success, and happiness.

I am the master of my thoughts and emotions.

I believe in my ability to create a better future.

I am motivated to achieve my highest potential.

I am grateful for the opportunities that come my way.

I am adaptable and can handle any situation.

I am constantly learning and growing.

I am guided by my inner wisdom and intuition.

I am a magnet for positive energy and people.

I am patient and trust in divine timing.

I am confident in my ability to make decisions.

I am focused on my goals with unwavering faith.

I am the captain of my ship, steering toward success.

I am motivated by the vision of my future self.

I am in tune with my inner desires and aspirations.

I am resilient and can overcome any adversity.

I am surrounded by love and support.

I am grateful for the progress I've made so far.

I am determined to turn my dreams into reality.

I am open to receiving all the good that life offers.

I am persistent, and my efforts are paying off.

I am confident in my ability to achieve greatness.

I am a beacon of positivity and inspiration.

I am constantly attracting opportunities for success.

I am aligned with my purpose and passion.

I am capable of handling any challenge that comes my way.

I am motivated by my inner sense of purpose.

I am on a path of continuous self-improvement and success.

Feel free to choose the affirmations that resonate most with you and incorporate them into your daily routine to boost your self-motivation and confidence.

Universe, grant me the strength to overcome challenges and achieve success.

May every step I take lead me closer to my goals.

I ask the universe for clarity and wisdom in my daily endeavors.

Let my actions be guided by purpose and passion.

Universe, help me to embrace change and adapt to new opportunities.

Grant me the courage to pursue my dreams without fear.

May I attract positive energy and abundance into my life.

I am open to receiving all the blessings the universe has in store for me.

Universe, align my thoughts and actions with my highest potential.

Let success flow effortlessly into my life.

Bless me with the patience to persist in the face of challenges.

I am grateful for the opportunities that come my way.

Universe, fill my heart with gratitude and positivity.

May my actions inspire and uplift others.

Help me to find balance and harmony in all aspects of my life.

Universe, guide me towards financial abundance and prosperity.

Let me radiate confidence and self-assurance.

I trust that the universe is conspiring in my favor.

May I attract supportive and loving relationships.

Universe, grant me the power to manifest my desires.

Help me release any doubts or limiting beliefs.

I am worthy of success, and I claim it with gratitude.

Universe, infuse my work with creativity and innovation.

Let me learn and grow from every experience.

May I be a beacon of positivity and optimism.

Grant me the ability to make wise decisions.

Universe, protect and guide me on my journey.

Help me to overcome any obstacles that arise.

I am open to receiving divine guidance and inspiration.

Let my intentions be clear and aligned with my purpose.

Universe, shower me with abundance and prosperity.

May I find joy and fulfillment in my daily life.

Bless me with good health and vitality.

I trust that the universe has a plan for my success.

Universe, help me to be of service to others.

Let me cultivate a mindset of abundance and gratitude.

May I be a source of positivity and love in the world.

Grant me the strength to persevere through challenges.

I am in tune with the abundant energy of the universe.

Universe, lead me towards opportunities for growth and expansion.

Help me to release any negative thoughts or doubts.

May my actions be aligned with my true purpose.

Bless me with financial prosperity and security.

I am open to receiving the gifts of the universe.

Universe, surround me with supportive and loving people.

Let me shine my light brightly for all to see.

Grant me the wisdom to make wise choices.

I trust in the divine timing of the universe.

Universe, guide me towards success in all areas of my life.

May I be a magnet for abundance, joy, and success.

Feel free to use these prayers as daily affirmations to help you focus your intentions and manifest success in your life.

ABOUT THE AUTHOR

From becoming a breakout star on his hit show *Creating Your Reality* on Law of Attraction Radio Network to becoming the bestselling author of *The Attractor Factor: The Key to Effortless Manifestation*, the man affectionately known as "Dr J" has quickly become Hollywood's foremost manifestation coach and advisor to the stars. With a celebrity clientele and a roster of clients in the world of business and finance, Dr. J is now considered by many to be one of the world's foremost leading authorities on Law of Attraction and is committed to helping you make your dreams a reality.

ADDITIONAL WORKS

The Attractor Factor: The Key to Effortless Manifestation

Law of Attraction Prayers for Healing

Life Your Way with Dr. J

NOTES

Made in the USA
Columbia, SC
18 May 2025